Gather Up the Fragments

[That None Be Lost]

By Rev. Cynthia Hill

PRESS

Gather Up the Fragments

Table of Contents

CHAPTER   PAGE

Preface xv

1. Out of Heartbreak Came Compassion 23
   Matthew 14: 12-14
   - Learning the discipline of solitude and prayer
   - Teaching and healing birthed from heartbreak
   - The hard shell is broken; tenderness emerges
   - Sharing the wealth of heaven
   - Transparency brings opportunity - Keep it real
   - Pain changes your focus
   - The sign of a surrendered life: "Its not about me"

2. Circumstances say "Send Them Away"- God says,
   "Serve Them" 42
   Matthew 14:15-16
   - Responding out of an earthly view
   - Common sense
   - Overwhelming numbers
   - Circumstances

- Time – when day appears to be almost gone
- Human ability
- Does God care about the spiritual and the natural
- Jesus says let them stay

3. But, We Don't Have What It Takes –
There's Much Too little...57
John 6: 5-6
- Jesus says, go and see
- Do you know who you are & what you have
- The Lord will provide'
- Stop being a lone ranger
- Jesus asks for your benefit- he knows
- Some may not notice your little but Jesus will
- Don't let your mind and mouth talk you out of what your faith has given you
- God doesn't want your human ability or human reasoning, but he does want you

4. Jesus says, "Bring what you have to me" 74
Matthew 14:19, Mark 6:39-40
- Jesus can make a feast in your desert
- Stop letting other define you; be an original
- But you've got to offer it up

5. Let Him Command Your Multitudes 104
Matthew 14:19
- Follow his instructions
- Learning to hear and obey
- You've got to keep a record
- He'll teach you how to put things in order in bite sized pieces
- From great to small - how to lead and to follow

6. God Gives Grace To The Humble – Sit Down! 131
   Mark 6:42
   - God cares where you sit – in green pastures
   - Know you're about to be fed and its gonna be good
   - When we sit at his feet he will make provision
   - Don't look for fame

7. Jesus Takes It With A Heavenly View.....................143
   Matthew 14:19
   - We're invited
   - Learning from the Master
   - The meaning of blessing
   - Keeping a heavenly view makes what seems impossible possible

8. Let Him Bless, Brake and Give It Back for Service.....160
   Mark 6:41; John 6:11
   - He has to bless it first
   - Learning to give thanks
   - Then comes the breaking
   - Some must be broken more than others
   - First the bread then the flesh
   - Now receive it back to share

9. Give It As He Gives It to You 178
   Mark 6:39
   - Follow his word
   - Follow his ways
   - Freely you received; freely give
   - Be willing and do serve
   - Don't get weary in well doing

10. Everybody Eats – Everybody Satisfied 188
    Mark 6:42
    - He offers it to everyone but only when we take it are we made full
    - Jesus didn't just whet the appetite nor did he tease them
    - He filled them to the full
    - There's a decision to be made
    - Will you receive what he offers

11. Gather Up the Fragments – Don't Lose Them 195
    John 6:12-13
    - What others left behind and discarded -lessons learned and abandoned
    - There's enough to fill your basket & enough for tomorrow
    - If it came from the hand of Jesus its blessed
    - You will need it again don't throw it away
    - Jesus doesn't desire any to perish
    - Remember men will be enlightened to see God's power and provision
    - You're needed to reflect on and reinforce the message
    - Breaking the curse by sharing the fragments

12. Jesus Doesn't Skip Women and Children 229
    Matthew 14:21
    - Why twelve baskets – foundations established
    - Jesus fed the men but he didn't neglect the women and children
    - Why were only the men counted
    - Countless women and children effected
    - Look at the effect of one: Adam, Abraham, Joseph, one little nameless boy, Jesus

About the Author 257

Dedicated to my beloved mother,

Vera L. Saulsberry

1935-2009

whose loving memory will always strengthen and inspire me.

Mom, was my biggest fan who always encouraged me to

put forth my very best in all that I did and to be forever

grateful for the many blessings God

has given to us!

Acknowledgements

First, I would like to thank my Lord and Savior Jesus Christ who gave his life for me and put the desire within me to share the words of this book. He is my salvation and my joy. All honor and glory belong to him for his great mercy, grace and strength!

My precious children, Valencia, Victoria, Vanessa and Vernon, their wonderful spouses and little ones have under-girded me with their tender love, strong support, and great faith in God. They never stopped believing in me and walked with me through all the struggles. Thanks for never tiring in listening to what I had to say, singing to me and praying for me.

I couldn't have done this without the support and confidence of my beloved sisters Kathy and Michele, who hold the love of Christ and the strength of our mom in their hearts. Thanks Dad and Lou for your love.

I thank God for my friend Frances with her unique way of challenging me to stick with it. Praise God for my family and many Christian friends who have listened to excerpts, encouraged and helped me to birth this project through many sincere prayers day and night. Thanks to Rev. Michele, Carolyn, Dr. Ernestine, Evangelist Dadzie, the Tousanas and Angel for your generosity and your prayers. Thanks to my friends at First Cathedral, Logan Street and Bethel House of Prayer for helping me to grow in grace.

Special thanks to my niece, Laura Farr, my friend Min. Cheryl Woods and Sis. Leatha Washington for reading, editing and giving valuable feedback on this manuscript. Thanks for encouraging me to get it published.

I thank my pastor, Dr. Nathaniel L. Edmond and the Second Baptist Church of Elgin for helping me to grow and for being a great encouragement to me. Without the love and faithful support of the members of Joy River Baptist Church, who exemplify the love of Christ in action, I could not have grown to the place of actually completing this manuscript. Thanks for letting me serve you. Since I began this book, three awesome women of faith have transitioned from here to glory my mom Vera, my grandmother Mary and my aunt Helen. Their love will always be in my heart and their warm encouragement in my memories.

PREFACE

A few years ago, while studying a passage of Scripture concerning the miracle of the Loaves and the Fishes for a sermon, the words "gather up the fragments that none be lost!" leaped off of the pages of my Bible and into my spirit. It was as if God was saying there is far more contained in these words for you than meets the naked eye. I felt compelled to take a closer look. The miracle happened one afternoon in Galilee when Jesus fed his disciples and five thousand men plus women and children on a meal that consisted of two fish and five barley loaves of bread. After the meal Jesus told his helpers to "Gather up the fragments that none be lost."

While meditating on those words, I began to think about the many broken people in the world and how Christ cared for them. My heart went out to the lonely, the displaced, the forgotten and the poor. For a long time I thought these alone represented the wounded and fragmented people God wanted to make whole. Certainly I didn't feel a part of that category. But as those words burned in my heart, I was inspired to dig a little deeper into the historical event surrounding those words. As I did, it took me on a personal journey of discovery and healing in the process. Perhaps you are wondering what can be learned from a story about an event that took place over 2000 years ago in a desert place near Galilee? What can be learned from a few tired men who found themselves surrounded by a mass of needy folks in need of much more than they possibly had to give. What an awkward situation had arisen in there lives! During that eventful afternoon the men find out some new things about themselves, the people and their teacher. While exploring the details and the message

of this great miracle, of the loaves and the fishes, I inter-
mingle some of my own life events, the truths and lessons
I've learned from the Lord along the way. I hope you too will
gather some fragments as you take this journey with me. The
biblical account of the story is found in: Matthew 14:12-21;
Mark 6:29-44; Luke 9:10-17 and John 6:1-14.

Gather Up The Fragments
That None Be Lost

Scriptures: Matthew 14:10-21, Mark 6:29-44,t
Luke 9:10-17, & John 6:1-14

The Gospel Accounts of the Miracle of the Fishes and the Loaves

Matthew 14:10-21

And he (Herod) sent, and beheaded John in the prison. And his head was brought in a charger, and given to the damsel: And she brought it to her mother. And his disciples came, and took up the body, and buried it, and went and told Jesus. When Jesus heard of it, he departed thence by ship into a desert place apart: and when the people had heard thereof, they followed him on foot out of the cities. And Jesus went forth, and saw a great multitude, and was moved with compassion toward them, and he healed their sick. And when it was evening, his disciples came to him, saying, This is a desert place, and the time is now past; send the multitude away, that they may go into the villages, and buy themselves victuals. But Jesus said unto them, They need not depart; give ye them to eat. And they say unto him, We have here but five loaves, and two fishes. He said, Bring them hither to me. And he commanded the multitude to sit down on the grass, and took the five loaves, and the two fishes, and looking up to heaven, he blessed, and brake, and gave the loaves to his disciples, and the disciples to the multitude. And they did all eat, and were filled: and they took up of the fragments that remained twelve baskets full. And they that had eaten were about five thousand men, beside women and children.

Mark 6:29-44

And when his disciples heard of it, they came and took up his corpse, and laid it in a tomb. And the apostles gathered themselves together unto Jesus, and told him all things, both what they had done, and what they had taught. And he said unto them, Come ye yourselves apart into a desert place, and rest a while: for there were many coming and going, and they had no leisure so much as to eat. And they departed into a desert place by ship privately. And the people saw them departing, and many knew him, and ran afoot thither out of all cities, and outwent them, and came together unto him. And Jesus, when he came out, saw much people, and was moved with compassion toward them, because they were as sheep not having a shepherd: and he began to teach them many things. And when the day was now far spent his disciples came unto him, and said, This is a desert place, and now the time is far passed:
Send them away, that they may go into the country round about, and into the villages, and buy themselves bread: for they have nothing to eat. He answered and said unto them, Give ye them to eat. And they say unto him, Shall we

go and buy two hundred pennyworth of bread, and give them to eat? He saith unto them, How many loaves have ye? Go and see. And when they knew, they say, Five, and two fishes. And he commanded them to make all sit down by companies upon the green grass. And they sat down in ranks, by hundreds and by fifties. And when he had taken the five loaves and the two fishes, he looked up to heaven, and blessed and brake the loaves, and gave them to his disciples to set before them; and the two fishes divided he among them all. And they did all eat, and were filled. And they took up twelve baskets full of the fragments, and of the fishes. And they that did eat of the loaves were about five thousand men.

Luke 9:10-17

And the apostles, when they were returned, told him all that they had done. And he took them, and went aside privately into a desert place belonging to the city called Bethsaida. And the people, when they knew it followed him: and he received them, and spake unto them of the kingdom of God, and healed them that had need of healing. And when the day began to wear away, then came the twelve, and said unto him, Send the multitude away, that they may go into the towns and country round about, and lodge, and get victuals: for we are here in a desert place. But he said unto them, Give ye them to eat. And they said, We have no more but five loaves and two fishes; except we should go and buy meat for all this people. For they were about five thousand men. And he said to his disciples, Make them sit down by fifties in a company. And they did so, and made them all sit down. Then he took the five loaves and the two fishes, and looking up to heaven, he blessed them, and brake, and gave to the disciples to set before the multitude. And they did eat, and were all filled: and there was taken up of fragments that remained to them twelve baskets.

John 6:1-14

After these things Jesus went over the sea of Galilee, which is the sea of Tiberias. And a great multitude followed him, because they saw his miracles which he did on them that were diseased. And Jesus went up into a mountain, and there he sat with his disciples.
And the Passover, a feast of the Jews, was nigh. When Jesus then lifted up his eyes, and saw a great company come unto him, he saith unto Philip, Whence shall we buy bread that these may eat? And this he said to prove him: for he himself knew what he would do. Philip answered him, Two hundred pennyworth of bread is not sufficient for them, that every one of them may take a little. One of the his disciples, Andrew, Simon Peter's brother, saith unto him, There is a lad here, which hath five barley loaves, and two small fishes: but what are they among so many? And Jesus said, Make the men sit down. Now there was much grass in the place. So the men sat down, in number about five thousand. And Jesus took the loaves and when he had given thanks, he distributed to the disciples, and the disciples to them that were set down; and like wise of the fishes as much as they would.When they were filled, he said unto his disciples, Gather up the fragments that remain, that nothing be lost. Therefore they gathered them together, and filled twelve baskets with the fragments of the five barley loaves, which remained over and above unto them that had eaten. Then those men, when they had seen the miracle that Jesus did, said, This is of a truth that prophet that should come into the world.

Out of Heartbreak Came Forth Compassion

Chapter 1

And his [John's] disciples came, and took up the body, and buried it, and went and told Jesus. When Jesus heard it, he departed thence by ship into a desert place apart...
Matthew 14:12-13

After just being rejected by his own hometown of Nazareth, Jesus then received the painful heartbreaking news that King Herod murdered his beloved cousin John. John had been born six months before Jesus. Their moms had stayed together for three months of their pregnancy. John, who became known as John the Baptist, had uncompromisingly stood for righteousness and as prophesied in Luke 1:17 fulfilled his divine calling:

"He turned the hearts of the Fathers to the children, and the disobedient to the wisdom of the just; to make ready a people prepared for the Lord."

John had reluctantly baptized his cousin Jesus in the Jordan. Then, through the revelation of the Holy Spirit, he announced Jesus' ministry: "...Behold the Lamb of God that taketh away the sin of the world," John 1:29. They had been close but now, John was dead – beheaded! Yes, Jesus was fully God, but also fully man. He was subject to the same feelings of sorrow and grief that we are. Isaiah the prophet says, "He is despised and rejected of men; a man of sorrows and acquainted with grief... Isaiah 53:3. The writer of Hebrews also reminds us of his familiarity with human emotions:

For we have not a High Priest who is unable to under-stand and sympathize and have a shared feeling with our infirmities and liability to the assaults of temptation, but One who has been tempted in every respect as we are, yet without sinning. Hebrews 4:15 AMP

I believe Jesus, in his infinite wisdom, pulled away to regroup and to be replenished by His Father. (Learning to attend to our physical and emotional need for rest is such a difficult lesson for most of us to learn.) He sought a place to reflect on the painful events instead of pressing on like nothing had happened. Have you ever had something so devastating happen in your life that it rocked your world, left your mind whirling, and your eyes stinging with tears? Before you knew it, the anxiety of the situation precipitated an intense headache, heartache and bewilderment. Have you ever been there? I have. But what's more heart-wrenching than seeing someone endure such painful grief is seeing someone who doesn't know when it is time to grieve! It's really sad to see someone receive the news about the loss of someone near and dear: a child, a spouse, a parent or a lover— but rather than be still to absorb the news, the person just presses on like nothing happened. Sometimes men and women simply refuse to allow themselves time to grieve. Rather than reflecting on what has just happened and what it means, the person begins to busy himself and to focus abnormally on some minute and unimportant detail. Subconsciously he is trying to stave off the inevitable torrent of painful emotions that simply must come. This is a disturbing sight because it is a futile exercise at maintaining control of his emotions. Unfortunately, it is an exercise with which I am quite familiar.

Oh, how vividly I recall the day when I received the courier-delivered papers announcing the request from the love of my life, from the father of my four children—requesting a divorce! How could this be? We had been high school sweethearts and married for many years. Sure, I knew he had found another new love, but wasn't this going to pass over like before? We had already withstood so many hurts, arguments, disappointments, personal and public humiliations during our marriage. Weren't we co-laborers in the gospel? How could this be happening? Weren't we committed "till death do us part"? I was stunned when I read those words, "petition for a divorce" until a deep blood-curdling scream broke the air and jarred me back to reality. At first, I didn't realize it had come from me. Then almost immediately like the pitiful sight I described earlier, I began to go into survival mode by commencing to compartmentalize my emotions.

That's just a fancy sounding phrase that means you put aside your real feelings because you are afraid and unwilling to deal with them. It is also called denial. Many of us have grown quite skilled at dealing with pain this way. At that time, I made up my mind to go into warrior mode. I was convinced that our marriage couldn't really be over. I would remain faithful to my children and fight to keep our home intact until my husband came to his senses. I would be faithful to my calling and to the church. I would complete my education plans by continuing to take classes until I received my degree. This divorce could not be happening. My self-denial of grief attitude continued for more than a year. I didn't realize until much later that I was trying to make things work out in my own strength. I was convinced that God had me in a protective bubble to keep me from breaking down. Despite all the talking, compromises, fasting and prayer, the twenty-nine year marriage finally came to an end. Our home was sold and our stuff divided. Friends with whom we had spent endless hours laughing and talking gradually shied away and faded off the scene. During this time, God graciously led me away to my own desert place. He led me to a great church in Connecticut, The First Cathedral, where I could begin to face my pain and begin to grieve toward healing. While living with my youngest daughter in Connecticut, I learned so many things about ministry, but most of all about *me*.

Jesus put men and women of God around me who could comfort but also challenge me. He helped me to learn to forgive and to reach out to others in my pain. God began to calm my raging sea of emotions and to teach me who I was. As I learned the discipline of solitude and prayer during my quiet time—and I had lots of quiet time to reflect— I soon had to face my why questions. Why did these things happen and why did they happen to me? I learned to become really honest with God in prayer. I learned to tell him how angry and disappointed I was with the situation and even with Him. During that time, I began to receive his two word answer to all my questions and complaints. "Trust Me!" Before all was said and done, I must admit those words became so frustrating to me because I wanted to be in control! But through it all, I became a more dedicated woman of prayer and I gained a deeper trust for God's sovereignty.

When we hurt deeply, God can finally break off the stuff that keeps us from plugging into him as our source. Then after the Master works with us a while, we can honestly say like David, "It is good for me that I have been afflicted; that I might learn thy statutes. Ps 119:71. Affliction is defined by Webster's dictionary as pain, suffering or great distress. The divorce from my husband certainly fit that definition in my life. Before I was afflicted with the crumbling of my little world, I had a bit of a hard shell and shallowness to my heart that would not let me care so much for people in a messy situation. I really didn't give much thought to how they had gotten into the situation they were in. I would, however, try to briefly analyze their plight to determine whether or not it was their fault. If it seemed like they were the victim, I could show more compassion, but if it was their doing, I sort of felt like they had earned their troubles. I know that's an ugly judgmental attitude, but that's where I was.

In the midst of a divorce and open shame, I found I had to face the music myself. I say my divorce was open shame because we lived as pastor and wife in a relatively small city and a lot of people knew our business. I had to face the fact that I too had to take responsibility for my part in the dissolution of our marriage. I had to learn to forgive myself for failing and falling short of my promise to God. That wasn't easy for me. I had vowed I would never make my family endure the pangs of divorce fallout as I had when I was growing up. Yes, God had already forgiven me according to his promise in James 1:9. *If we confess our sins, he is faithful and just to forgive us our sins and to cleanse us from all unrighteousness.* Forgiving myself, however, was a very slow process. It took me about five years. Through it all, I began to gain a deeper understanding of God's grace. By the loving support of my family members and my extended family in Christ, I experienced much mercy and undeserved favor. The Lord Jesus taught me to understand that, although people are hurting sometimes because of some bad choices, he still loves them, wants to help them and really wants to heal their lives. So, enduring deep pain personally helped me to break off the hard shell of self-righteousness and to bring out more tenderness in me.

It seemed that when I became more broken and allowed myself to weep the most, God opened doors for me to minister to really broken people. I was given opportunities to minister to women in prison, to minister to women whose lives had been ravaged by rape, rejection, drugs and A.I.D.S. I met and ministered to little children and to many people who were struggling with unforgiveness. During this time, I began to learn a new level of compassion and not just pity or tolerance. Satan meant the hurtful things of our past to destroy us, but God can use them for our ultimate good. There used to be a time I simply refused to show my weaknesses or even to admit God had to help me over a struggle. By becoming broken, I became more transparent. By becoming more transparent, God kept giving me opportunities to minister to those in need. At these times, I felt most fulfilled and focused on the purpose God had for my life.

I think for the first time in my life, I realized the powerful truth of this scripture found in the book of Ephesians: *"For we are his workmanship, created in Christ Jesus unto good works, which God hath before ordained that we should walk in them"* Ephesians 2:10.

My focus changed and I actually started to realize it wasn't all about me. Remember Matthew 14: Jesus had pulled aside to rest and reflect with his disciples because he was emotionally drained and his disciples, just returning from their missionary journey, were also sapped. Jesus had previously sent the disciples out by twos after empowering them to preach, heal and to cast out devils. Now they had returned tired, but excited, proud and anxious to tell Jesus all that they had done. So Jesus, though mourning the loss of his cousin John the Baptist, focused on them and patiently listened to their excited recounting of the things they had done and taught. In my mind I could see this scene as being much like a weary parent who has just arrived home after a rough day at work. She tries to gently calm down her child as she patiently listens to his breathless account of some exciting news about an event that took place at school or about a brand new friend he has just met that day. In the same way, Jesus listened and urged them to come aside to a deserted place to rest awhile. He could give of himself because he knew his purpose and he knew it wasn't about him or even about his feelings at the moment.

That's a sign of a truly surrendered life. Jesus had gathered up his fatigued disciples in the midst of his personal pain and attempted to exit to a place of solitude and restoration. But the Scriptures record that a crowd caught a glimpse of their retreat and raced on ahead on foot to the other side of the lake. The crowd was spiritually hungry, desperate and in need of healing. We can't blame the crowd for being insensitive. They didn't know what Jesus was feeling. They didn't suspect that the disciples were weary. Like most of us, when we have a desperate need, we become single-mindedly focused on getting our needs met. They had heard that Jesus had done good things for others and that he had the words of life. Although we have become so accustomed to the availability of Scripture and the word preached through television and radio, these people did not know if this would be their one and only chance to hear and to see Jesus. As a result they were determined to seize the moment and not let opportunity slip past them. How did Jesus respond to this intrusion? Was it with disgust, annoyance or indifference? No! He did not see the crowd as an intrusion, but quite the opposite.

I just love this next verse in Matthew, which says: *And Jesus went forth, and saw a great multitude and was moved with compassion toward them, and he healed their sick. Matthew 14:14.* The phrase 'moved with compassion' meant he felt deep heartfelt empathy and sympathy for the needs of the people who had gathered around him. As a result, he healed them spiritually with the preached word of the gospel and he healed them physically in their bodies with the touch

35

of his hand. I am convinced God wants to use us to do the same, but we are not usable until we, like Jesus, give him our heartbreak by faith and allow him to replace it with compassion. That transfer can only occur when we are willing to admit that 1) it really happened, 2) it really hurt and 3) our heavenly Father loves us and is able to heal the pain.

Finally, to be able to get on with Life, we must be willing to let the pain go. We must stop carrying it around with us as a keepsake that we frequently pull out and fondle whenever we feel like having a pity party. Nor can we wear it on our faces like someone wearing a victory medal on their chest. The only difference is that this medal, shouts to the world,

> *We must stop carrying it [pain] around with us as a keepsake that we frequently pull out and fondle whenever we feel like having a pity party.*

"I've been wronged; pity me!" Let's face it. If you have lived any time on this earth you know that, beyond a fleeting interest, most people are too wrapped up in their own problems to care for too long about yours. And even if they do care, there is very little they can do about it. So looking to people to remove your misery generally compounds the feelings of victimization and rejection. People just can't fix it. As Jesus healed the crowd spiritually, emotionally and physically many years ago, he is still doing the same today. Jesus' healing is available today for all who are willing to let those destructive feelings and thoughts go.

We each have a part to play in our own deliverance, however. Too often we want someone else to do everything for us while we sit like a bump on a log and do nothing. Therefore, we keep wandering around and around aimlessly in the same old mess for years. We are unable to grow strong and to go out and grasp what God wants to give us. God has made a promise to all who put their trust in him to restore all the years that were stolen from them by the enemy, Satan, but we have to be willing to get into position to receive it. We must trust him to live again:

And I will restore to you the years that the locust hath eaten, the cankerworm, and the caterpillar, and the palmerworm, my great army which I sent among you. And ye shall eat in plenty, and be satisfied, and praise the name of the Lord your God, that hath dealt wondrously with you: and my people shall never be ashamed.

Joel 2:25-26

Even a worm or a bug, one of God's smallest creatures, refuses to just wallow and die if you chop off a tail or a leg. They will grow a new tail and keep on moving or at the very least keep trying to survive until there is no life left inside of them. I am ashamed to say I was stuck in depression for such a long time. Instead of practicing songs of worship and praise, I rehearsed the sing-song words "poor little ol' me", "but God I don't understand" and "why me?". In other words: pity party. But thanks to learning the discipline of solitude and prayer, really meditating on God's Holy Word and receiving lots of loving help to get rid of a wilderness mindset, I gained inner strength and joy. God has changed much of my crying into praising and dancing. I still occasionally have a pity party, but I refuse to stay there. The longer you allow yourself to mope around in self-pity and despair, the harder it is to break free from its grip.

Just as it is unhealthy to deny that the blow of suffering you received was real, so is it unhealthy to wallow in self-pity for too long. Sometimes I thought despair was glued to me and I would never get free. At times, I became terrified that I was going to lose my sanity and never come back to the land of the living. Some of us can become too skilled at grieving losses. Then we become unreceptive to life and joy and we can suck the life out of anyone who hangs around us too long. In fact, sometimes we can mourn the death of a loved one so long that we nearly join them. There is a time for mourning, but it must eventually come to an end. *"To everything there is a season, a time for every purpose under heaven,"* Ecclesiastes 3:1. I am convinced that a mind can only tolerate sad depressing thoughts for so long before the effects begin to manifest in the physical body. The negative thoughts leave us open to sickness and disease—just what Satan wants. Remember, the thief Satan came to steal your joy, kill your hope and destroy your future, but Jesus Christ came to give you life and to give it to you to the full. That is the promise of the Lord—abundant life!

God has so many good thoughts and plans for each and every one of his children including you. He has already given me glimpses of some of the awesome things he wants to do through my life. My job is to receive, to believe, to hold on to and to act on the promises and dreams until they fully come to pass. One of the things God wants me to do is to reach out to hurting people and share the message of hope and life in Jesus Christ. Through my personal heartbreak, Christ has shown me compassion and he has also shown me purpose. Through healing and teaching me, he gave me hope for a better future. I am glad that through suffering, the Lord helped me shed a lot of my plastic veneer so that I could become the person he intended for me to be. Of course, I am still a work in progress, but I am ready to go forward on the journey. How about you?

Let's recap some things learned:

- Out of heartbreak the hard shell is broken and tender-ness emerges.

- The discipline of solitude and prayer brings strength

- Transparency brings opportunity to minister

- A new focus emerges: compassion not self-pity

- Learning it's not about me is the sign of a surrendered life

- God's healing and teaching bring about hope

Send Them Away?

Chapter 2

And when it was evening, his disciples came to him, saying, This is a desert place, and the time is now past, send the multitude away, that they may go into the villages, and buy themselves victuals. But Jesus said unto them, they need not depart; give ye them to eat. Matthew 14: 15-16

I t never ceases to amaze me how reluctant I am to relinquish my old earthly, sensual way of thinking in order to grasp a heavenly view. Of course it is quite easy to stay focused on the earthly realm considering we live on the Earth. We live in a body made of earth and our senses are subject to the physical. But if we have been born again from above by believing in and receiving Jesus Christ as our Lord and Savior, we are called to change our perspective. To say it another way, God is calling his children to cease living by just what they can see, hear, smell, taste, touch or even reason. He wants us to live in this world, but to not succumb to the world's lullaby or system of thinking. I believe we'll see this fact evidenced as we continue to delve into the riches of this miraculous historical event performed by Jesus.

In Matthew chapter fourteen, verse fifteen our scene opens with the words, "And when it was evening..." Apparently, it was noticeably growing late in the day. Anyone could see that the hour was growing late. The sun was hanging low in the sky and the shadows were growing long. Perhaps you could hear the growing sounds of crickets conversing and the deep rumbling tones that empty stomachs make. A quick span of the

> *We live in a body made of earth and our senses are subject to the sensual. But if we have been born again from above by believing in and receiving Jesus Christ as our Lord and Savior, we are called to change our perspective.*

terrain with the naked eye reported a lack of amenities and especially a noticeable absence of food sources. As a matter of fact, in close proximity there was nothing visible but dirt, grass and a lot of hungry faces. Looming in the distance, there were some villages and the Sea of Galilee. The first might offer lodging and both places offered the possibility of food, if only it wasn't so late. With great concerns about the circumstances and conditions, the disciples viewed Jesus as being preoccupied with teaching and healing, but unaware of how badly this situation could get out of hand. After all there were only twelve of them with Jesus facing a seemingly numberless sea of faces. All that he was saying and doing sounded, looked and felt good, but something had better be done quickly or they would have a mess on their hands.

Common sense dictated a need to get these people in a position to take care of their hunger before it grew too late for them to find a place to eat and rest. After all, the disciples were only doing what comes naturally. Nothing is wrong with common sense. This good sense is generally available to all mankind for the purpose of assessing a situation and drawing a rational conclusion. So, the disciples respectfully said to Jesus, "Excuse us Master, we are sure you haven't noticed, but this is a desert place with no restaurants or hotels nearby. It will be getting dark soon and there are a whole lot of people out here. These people will probably look to us to take care of their physical needs as well as the spiritual soon and Jesus we just don't have it like that! Master, we've discussed the situation among ourselves and we've concluded that you should send them away now. If they are lucky, they can get to a nearby town before too late and fend for themselves for food and lodging."

The disciples' suggestion was quite logical based on human reasoning and perception, but they soon found out it wasn't acceptable by the standards of the Lord of the Universe. Incredulously, Jesus turned and calmly responded to their caring but reasonable suggestion with words that basically said, "No, there is no urgency or need for them to leave. Let them stay and you give them something to eat!" Now in all fairness, I am sure the disciples panicked because this looked like an impossible situation that had suddenly gone from bad to worse. Not daring to openly question Jesus' instructions, they probably thought to themselves that his words were a bit absurd. They must have thought, "Didn't he understand what we just said? What is he trying to do? We cannot possibly feed all these hungry people."

Have you ever faced what seemed like an impossible situation by all human standards and God seemed to be saying, "trust me you can do it"? In those times, you can look at all the possible angles and the problem still looks the same—too big! You add and re-add the figures, but they just won't add up. You try not to think about it or squint real hard at it, but the situation just won't seem to go away. Yet somehow if you are a Christian, you still hear deep within your spirit the words, "only believe". When I was seventeen years old and a fairly new Christian, I had just such a situation to occur. Once again I had procrastinated getting out of the house on time for my first period class. That summer our family had moved to the far south side of Chicago just prior to the beginning of my senior year at Lindblom Technical High School. Unfortunately, I had already been tardy twice during the semester and a third time would mean an automatic suspension from school. However, being suspended was totally out of the question! My mom had made sure I was awakened in plenty of time to get ready for school. She busied herself with helping my younger siblings to get ready for school before she had to leave for work herself. She said I was responsible enough to catch the bus and subsequent trains needed to get me to school on time. Unlike many of us parents today, my mom believed in raising independent children and she didn't believe in bailing us out of jams that we got ourselves into. So, I couldn't expect to get a ride to school just to keep me from being late. Well, I had cut it real close again and try as I might to run with all my books for the city bus, I missed it. The next bus came along a few minutes later as I continued to pray, "Please help me God. I can't be late because I will get suspended. Then I can't return to school without my mom having to miss work, come up to the school and get me reinstated. Besides that I will have a black mark on my school record." We were raised to believe that negative stuff on your records—grammar school, high school, work—followed you to the grave. Needless to say, I was really motivated to seek God for the miraculous.

I had recently been reading in the Bible that if we had faith the size of a grain of mustard seed, we could ask what we wanted and it would be done for us. Missing a single bus may not seem like such a big deal, but you must understand it had a domino effect. You see I had to take a city bus to the elevated train station located at 95th street and the Dan Ryan Expressway. Then I had to take the "A" train to the 63rd street elevated train station. Then I had to catch one more bus at the end of the train line to take me to Wolcott where the school was located. The A and the B trains ran alternately so if you missed the "A" train, the "B" didn't make a stop at 63rd street and you could be over an hour late getting to school. I kept praying against all reason that God would somehow get me to school on time. I thought maybe the bus would travel real fast and miss a few stops in order to get me to the train on time, but it didn't happen that way. As a matter of fact, as I got off the bus and dropped my token into the turnstile, my train pulled off from the station platform. As I plodded down the stairs to the platform I kept praying, "God I know you're going to help me. I don't know how Father, but I know you can and you will." Of course I had confessed my sin already and ask for forgiveness. Well as I got to the edge of the platform to look for the next train which I knew would be a "B" train anyway, I saw nothing coming toward the station yet. Then I turned the other way looking up the track in the direction of the train I had just missed. To my surprise, the train was backing down the track to the platform where I was standing. I didn't see a conductor looking out of the window. Not that anyone would back up a train for me anyway. But nevertheless the train backed up and the doors flew open. I walked in with my mouth hanging wide-open. Not one person looked up from their papers or even seemed surprised at this strange turn of events. I sat mind-boggled all the way from 95th to 63rd street before I could finally get the words thank you Lord out of my mouth. Believe it or not, I made my connecting train on time and arrived a few minutes early for school. I told everyone about it at school that Friday morning and I even rehearsed the events to my Sunday school class at church. My Sunday school teacher responded that I must be one of God's chosen people or something because the "L" trains don't back up for anyone in Chicago.

Actually my teacher was right because every believer has been chosen by God. Ephesians 1:4 says:

"...even as [in his love] He chose us [actually picked us out for Himself as His own] in Christ before the foundation of the world, that we should be holy (consecrated and set apart for Him) and blameless in His sight, even above reproach, before Him in love". AMP

At the time, I didn't even know this scripture, but I knew that my heavenly Father loved me and cared about me. I insisted to the class that I wasn't any more important than anyone else, but I was convinced that God would do the impossible for any of his kids if we would just believe. So often, when God does things out of the ordinary people try to make it seem like God will only do miraculous things for a select few, as if the person who received the blessing deserved the credit, rather than God. All the praise and glory belongs to God because he is good and merciful. He acts on the behalf of those who trust and believe in Him.

Ye are my witnesses, saith the Lord, and my servants whom I have chosen: that ye may know and believe me, and understand that I am he: before me there was no God formed, neither shall there be after me. Isaiah 43:10

My miracle didn't line up with common sense or even with human rationalization, but it did attest to the limitless ability of God. It taught me that God cares about both the spiritual and the natural things in Life. Jesus cared about the multitudes' spiritual needs as well as their physical ones too. He had already demonstrated that fact through his healing of their sick bodies, but he knew that they had a need for simple nourishment also. Too often we see our God as too small just like the disciples did in this case. We think he cannot possibly be aware of what's going on in our little lives while he's taking care of the rest of the planet and the Universe. We forget that he takes care of the birds of the air and the lilies of the field.

During my train miracle, God reassured me that what is important to me is also important to him. The Bible says that God is no respecter of persons; therefore I know that all of us are important to him. He wants to do fantastic things in our lives if we are willing to change our focus from the mundane to the realization that we as believers are truly seated in heavenly places in Christ Jesus (Colossians 2:6). In the natural, it may even appear to be getting late in the evening of your life. You may feel like you are getting too old for God to use you in this world. You may think it's too late for you to change your viewpoint or it's too late to learn new things assome say, "it's too late to teach an old dog a new trick". I know that thought crossed my mind. But God is calling us to look toward him in faith believing that with God all things are possible.

> *It is so much easier to trust what we can see, feel, smell, taste and touch than it is to trust the goodness and love of an invisible God.*

Like the disciples, we have short memories and refuse to put two and two together. Before this day, the disciples had already seen Jesus perform several miracles. He had already turned 120 gallons of water into 120 gallons of world-class wine. They had seen him open blinded eyes, un-stop deaf ears, put flesh back on a leprous man's body and stop a funeral processional to bring the deceased back to life. But for some strange reason, like us, the disciples had a hard time believing Jesus wouldn't be stumped or overwhelmed by such large numbers or by some new thing they hadn't seen before. Each miracle seemed disconnected and had no bearing on the next in the disciple's viewpoint. Just because Jesus could calm a raging sea didn't mean he could tame growling stomachs! Just because he could call forth fish to fill fishing nets so full that the boats began to sink, didn't mean he could fill and satisfy this many hungry people in a desert place! It is so much easier to trust what we can see, feel, smell, taste and touch than it is to trust the goodness and love of an invisible God. But like the disciples, Jesus who has already proven himself over and over again is calling for our perspective to change no matter what situation is facing us. He is more than able to handle and help us to succeed in whatever dilemma we face. The challenges we face may be external or they may be internal. We may have a mountain of debt, a difficult marriage, a troubled child or we may have a deadly disease.

We may be emotionally crippled by past hurts and disap-

pointments. We may have made some terrible choices in the

past that have cost us our freedom, family, finances and

peace of mind. God is

> *The ultimate purpose of miracles is that man would through faith in Christ Jesus escape the deserved wrath of God, live life abundantly and glorify God the Father.*

more than able and

willing to come to our

rescue, but we have to

choose to shift our view

from our limitations and those of others to the limitless

ability of Jehovah God. We have to realize that we have

access, through faith in his Son Jesus Christ, to limitless

resources to accomplish the will of God in the earth. God

doesn't do the miraculous in our lives, however, just to sat-

isfy our own selfish whims like some spiritual Santa Claus.

To the contrary, he demonstrates his love and what we call

miracles to fulfill his will and his purposes.

The ultimate purpose of miracles is that man would escape the deserved wrath of God, live life abundantly and glorify God the Father through faith in Christ Jesus. Jesus came after all for that express purpose.

"For the Son of Man is come to seek and to save that which was lost." (Luke 19:10) The greatest miracle in anyone's life is just that: Salvation. Through God's grace by faith in Jesus, a change takes place in the heart of one who is dead in trespasses and sin. He is changed into a brand new creation in Christ. We can only experience the fullness of victorious living by faith with a mind that has been renewed by the Word of God. As we continue to dig deeper into this particular miracle of the loaves and fishes and as we gather up the fragments of God's workings in our own lives, I am sure the Holy Spirit will give us a renewed mindset about the Lord and his ability to transform our lives and the lives of others.

But We Don't Have What It Takes; There's Too Little!

Chapter 3

'Shedding the victim's mindset'

...he saith unto Philip, where shall we buy bread, that these may eat. And this he said to prove him: for he himself knew what he would do. (John 6:5-6) He saith unto them, "How many loaves have ye? go and see."(Mark 6:38) There is a lad here, which hath five barley loaves and two fishes: but what are they among so many?(John 6:9)

O f course we believe in the power of God. You and I probably wouldn't blink an eye at the statement that Jesus can do anything. But, if you are talking about doing it through us, we say, that's a totally different situation". For some reason, when we begin to entertain the idea that God may have some specific purpose in mind for us or that he may desire to use us to fulfill his will and plan on earth, we begin to quickly back up into the corner of doubt and fear. Why is that? How is it possible for us to say in one breath that we have great confidence in the ability, wisdom and generosity of God, who is our Father (if we have received his Son, Jesus), but we have so little confidence in ourselves? Is it possible that we don't really know who we are? Or better yet, maybe we don't know whose we are? Deep down inside, maybe we think that when God uses someone to do his work, some of the ability lies within the person. Therefore, when we are asked to do something like talk to a friend or neighbor about Christ, we can quickly say, "no, I can't do that. I don't have what it takes. I don't know enough. I don't have enough courage." Now, I can't point a scolding finger

> *I think God always challenges us with dreams and requests that are beyond our comfort zones because he wants us to realize our sufficiency lies in him and in him alone.*

at anyone else for having a lack of self- confidence because there are literally three fingers pointing back at me. I think God always challenges us with dreams and requests that are beyond our comfort zones because he wants us to realize our sufficiency lies in him and in him alone. Jesus continually reminds us that we must always realize who he is and stay connected to him in order to produce anything lasting and of value. John 15:5 records Jesus as saying, "I am the Vine, ye are the branches: he that abideth in me, and I in him, the same bringeth forth much fruit: for without me ye can do nothing." I believe God wants us to mature to a place of abiding trust in him and in his ability to equip us for what-ever challenges may face us. The word 'abide' means to stay; to remain; to live; to dwell or to be in a state that begins and continues. Our tendency is to make frequent visits to Christ, but to mainly abide in ourselves and trust in our own ingenuity. Jesus challenges us to actually choose to abide in him. 'To abide in Christ' means to follow his example of living a life of complete reliance and trusting obedience to the will of God. The Scriptures illuminate the fact that the disciples, who walked daily with Christ, struggled with this same issue of abiding, just as we do.

The miracle of the fish and loaves appears in all four Gospel accounts, but each contains just a little additional information to enlighten us about the event and

> *Our tendency is to make frequent visits to Christ, but to mainly abide in ourselves and trust in our own ingenuity.*

the people involved in it. Up until now we have been focusing on the account as written in the book of Matthew, but I'd like to take a quick trip to passages in the book of John and the book of Mark to look at the issue of the insufficiency that accompanies an independent attitude. In the sixth chapter of the book of John, we find the words "he [Jesus] saith unto Philip, Whence shall we buy bread that these may eat? And this he said to prove him for he himself knew what he would do". Jesus specifically singled out Philip to ask him where they could purchase food for all the people who were gathered around them. Before we can dwell too long on that question, John inserts the comment that Jesus had asked Philip this question for the purpose of testing him. So why did Jesus suddenly change or "flip the script" on poor Philip? In a gentle shepherd-like manner, he had been freely doling out instruction and doing healing miracles all day long for the crowd, but now the text clearly says he was testing Philip! Had Philip done something wrong? No, the Scriptures don't indicate any wrongdoing on Philip's part. Philip who was representative of the other eleven disciples had been with Jesus from the beginning and had seen him work time and time again. Philip along with the other eleven had recently returned from a successful mission trip where he and the others had been given clear instructions and empowerment to carry them out. In the same way that we are given an exam for a particular academic subject in order to test our level of understanding and comprehension, the Lord was now testing Philip and his disciple brothers to see if they had learned well the lesson about

"who was the Source of their supply". He wanted to see if

> *He (God) tests or proves us not to see us fail, but to mature us to perfection.*

they would trust him or revert back to self-sufficiency as usual. Just as he did with Philip, God often places the same test upon our lives.

He already knows what he is going to do before he allows

that situation to arise in our lives. The question is do we

know enough to turn to him and to trust him for guidance

and provision. He tests or proves us not to see us fail, but to

mature us to perfection.

When I was a kid there was a television show about a

superhero called the Green Hornet. He had a side-kick, Cato,

who was forever waiting in some obscure place to pounce on

the unsuspecting Green Hornet. By doing this repeatedly he

was testing the Hornet's ability to properly react to an ene-

my's surprise attack. Cato knew the Hornet was capable, but

he helped to build his confidence and skill by testing him

through various angles and conditions. Likewise, Jesus allows tests into our lives. In this case he tested Philip because he needed the disciples to know where their source of provision lay. Unfortunately Philip, like us, reverted back to faithlessly looking to human ability and reasoning for a resolution to the problem. Jesus wasn't surprised, however, because he knew what he was planning to do and he also knew how Philip would react. Philip looked at himself, at the treasury purse and he looked at the size of the crowd to conclude that there just wasn't enough money to feed all those people. He forgot or was not aware that he was standing before Jehovah-Jireh, the God who provides and the God who has more than enough. He didn't realize that he had connections and could ask Jesus for what was needed. So often we too get overwhelmed and discouraged because we don't realize who we are as children of God. Nor do we utilize by faith the awesome privilege of asking or making our request confidently known to God in prayer. Too frequently we run around trying everybody and everything else before coming to God with a defeated attitude. I often hear people finally say, "Well all we can do now is pray." Instead, that should be the first thing we do. Jesus, being the excellent teacher that he is, continued to give his disciples an opportunity to learn through the experience. In Mark 6:37 the Scriptures indicate Jesus asked the entire group of disciples, "How many loaves do you have?" Then he told them to go and see. Repeatedly throughout the bible we find God using the most minute or unusual things we possess to affect some great victory in our lives. He used David's slingshot and one

> *God will always expect us to take inventory of what we already have. He wants us to take what is familiar and surrender it to him for transformation.*

smooth stone to bring down the giant Goliath. He used torches inside clay pots and the voices of Gideon's 300 men to overthrow a host of thousands. He used the staff of Moses to break Pharaoh's tyranny and to divide the Red Sea. At one time God literally asked Moses, "what is that in your hand...

" (Exodus 4:2). Jesus was pretty much saying the same thing

to the disciples when he said 'go and see what food is in your

possession'. God will always expect us to take inventory of

what we already have. He wants us to take what is familiar

and surrender it to him for transformation. In this case provi-

sion was going to be perfected through someone else's lunch.

Too often we think that we have to be a lone ranger. We feel

too proud to let anyone know we need help and often end up

like the toddler who says, "I do it myself!" and then walk

around in shoes on the wrong feet. Jesus wants us to learn

that it is not about us. The plan is to do the will of God and for

God to get the glory. That means that we can't successfully

do the work of God in our own strength and that we most

often will need the help of other believers. Can't you imagine

all the disciples checking amongst themselves to see who

hadn't eaten all of their lunch yet only to discover nothing

was left but empty lunch baskets? Then can you further picture them being a bit embarrassed to have to ask the crowd if

anyone had any bread or any food? With eyes spanning the

crowd, the disciples finally hear a little voice say, "I didn't eat

my lunch yet." "You can have it." You remember, the disci-

ples had a little impatience issue with children being brought

to Jesus in these gatherings anyway. They had shown that at

another gathering when they rebuked parents for bringing up

their children to be blessed by Jesus. I think they may have

felt like some adults of old felt, 'children should be seen but

not heard.' Thank God the Lord sees things differently. In

several Gospel accounts Jesus admonishes the disciples to

"suffer [allow] the little children to come unto me because of

such is the kingdom of heaven." (Matthew 19:14, Mark 10:4

& Luke 18:16). Although the two little fishes and five loaves

are mentioned in all four gospels, only John tells us that they

were obtained from the hand of a young boy. Perhaps it

wasn't an important detail to most of the disciples or even to

the crowd in the big scheme of things, but it was important to

God and he had the youngest of the disciples to tell us about it. Even the offerings we consider meager and insignificant mean much to God! He made sure that John, the Gospel writer who focused on the deity and character of Jesus, recorded the fact that a young lad supplied the meal to be used by the Lord. Nothing escapes the eye of God, definitely not an act of kindness. He said as much in the following passage of scripture:

> *...and He that receiveth me receiveth him that sent me. He that receiveth a prophet in the name of a prophet shall receive a prophet's reward; and he that receiveth a righteous man shall receive a righteous man's reward. And whosoever shall give to drink unto one of these little ones a cup of cold water only in the name of a disciple, verily I say unto you, he shall in no wise lose his reward.*
> *Matthew 10:40-42*

Others may not notice or give you credit for what you do for the Lord, but it will never go un-noticed nor unrewarded by him.

Returning to our text in John chapter 6, we find Andrew advising Jesus that they have been blessed to receive a little boy's picnic lunch as a contribution to the cause. Did you notice? It isn't Philip, but Andrew who brings the little boy's lunch to Jesus. One might be tempted to say Andrew was able to locate the provision because he had greater faith than Philip. After all, when Jesus had asked Philip where to get bread, he responded that even 200 pennyworth (a whole year's wages) of bread couldn't feed all these people. But before we start singing Andrew's praises, realize that the tendency to rely upon self and to doubt the ability of God to provide is a universal problem. The scripture says that almost before he could get the details of the blessing out of his mouth, he allows doubt to form his next few words which are, "but what are they among so many?" By faith and obedience he and the other disciples had located a person willing to freely share his substance with the Master for the needs of the masses. But then, like many of us, he allowed negative thoughts and negative talk to overtake the joy of the provision of God. The Bible says that "death and life are in the power of the tongue..."(Proverbs 18:21). In other words, we'll have the results or fruit of the words we believe and say. I know I personally have struggled much with keeping my mind and mouth from talking me out of the things my faith has already given me. I started to say the things my faith has promised me, but I am compelled to say instead "my faith has given me" because when we receive a thing by faith it is actually fact even before it is manifested. We must just be careful to nurture that promise with thoughts and words of faith to keep ourselves from moving out of the place where God can bless us. God doesn't want our excuses and doubt. He works with faith. So, if we are to experience the fullness of God's blessings, we must be careful not to surround ourselves with negative unbelieving people, and we must also refrain from thinking and saying negative things ourselves.

Jesus is quite capable of taking our little and increasing it into much. He is our Creator and he can actually make something out of nothing. But, in his wisdom he allows us to share in the process so that we remember that God works through people. He has chosen to work through us. He finances the Kingdom, wins the lost, encourages the broken-hearted, makes disciples and heals the sick through us. God is looking for a willing vessel who is connected and full of faith to use today to show a dying world the message of grace. The Lord is personally challenging each of us to go and see what he has given us to work with in promoting the Kingdom. He wants us to learn who we are according to the Word of God and to learn who we belong to according to the Scriptures. He is inviting us to be born again and to learn to abide, to stay connected to him. He is inviting us to learn to be continually dependent upon him and not on

> *We can generally tell where our heart is by the things that come out of our mouths.*

our human ability or human reason. He wants you and me to live by faith because he doesn't honor excuses or doubt. He loves us and has a wonderful plan for our lives that will be executed by faith. The well known faith decree found in Hebrews 11:1 states, "Now faith is the substance of things hoped for, the evidence of things not seen". Therefore, it is imperative that we learn not to allow our thoughts and words to talk us out of the things our faith in Christ has already acquired for us. There are things God has laid up for us which we have yet to see, but we must agree with him in heart and mind before we can receive them. We can generally tell where our heart is by the things that come out of our mouths. Jesus said, "...for of the abundance of the heart his mouth speaketh." (Luke 6:45)

Keep in mind that the things God has for us are not limited to mere material possession, but rich spiritual blessings as well. Such things as love, joy, faith, peace, patience, self-control, gentleness, goodness and boldness to share the good news of the Gospel are a few examples. Sometimes however, it is easier to measure the tangible ones. That's why testimonies of material blessings are so frequently shared. It is easier for people to validate that the blessing was actually received. For instance, I remember when we were looking to move out of our starter home located in a suburban Ghetto into a bigger one located in a safer neighborhood. I had heard a minister on the radio teach that we should be specific when we asked God for blessings. He said we should list or write the requests out on paper, ask for them in prayer and agree with God that we believe he will bless us with the request. Well with my second home and even with this latest one, I did just that. As long as I was hesitant to verbalize what I believed God wanted me to have I did not receive it. It stayed a fuzzy distant hope in my heart, but soon after I committed my request to God in prayer by faith, he brought all the necessary components together to bless me. I had to believe and be willing to obey his instructions regarding giving, spending and trusting, and he brought it to pass. I received what I had requested even with such specific details as laundry chutes, dressers that were built into the wall, a fireplace and more. Our heavenly Father delights in blessing us if we will only learn to trust him and put everything in his secure capable hands.

Jesus Says, "Bring What You Have To Me!"

Chapter 4

And they said unto him, we have here but five loaves and two fishes. He said, Bring them hither to me.

Matthew 14:17-18

"What can he do with this little bit of food?" they thought. The disciples had scratched their heads and exhausted their intellect trying to determine the best way to serve even a little appetizer to this huge crowd. Jesus seemed indifferent to their suggestion to take the 200 pennies (approximately $40 in today's economy) from the treasury bag to purchase as much bread as possible. Instead he had sent them to look among the crowd to see what bread they already had. Now that they had come back with the report of having found a little child's lunch consisting of five barley loaves and two small fishes, he seemed content and not the least bit troubled. Instead of letting them in on his plan, he simply had said, "bring them here to me". What's that all about? What can he do with these groceries?

Jesus knew exactly what he was doing when he said to the disciples, "...bring them here to Me", (Matthew 14:17 AMP). Again, like us, their focus was on the things they could see without regard for the hands of God. So they didn't get it. He was asking for more than a mere transfer of goods or groceries. He was requesting a transfer of trust. He was asking for a transfer from self-sufficiency to Christ-dependency. He had allowed them to thoroughly exhaust their own ability to bring them to a place of demonstration. He wanted them to put all their stuff into his hands. He wanted them to give up their plans for the meager lunch and to entrust it to him for his use.

Years ago, there was a song published by a Christian artist name "Evie" entitled "Give them all to Jesus". The chorus went like this:

Give them all; Give them all; Give them all to Jesus
Shattered dreams and wounded hearts and broken toys
Give them all; Give them all; Give them all to Jesus
And he will turn your sorrows into joys.

Sometimes that is one of the hardest things for us to do as adults. We cling to our broken pieces so dearly because we feel they are all we have left. This is a sign of broken and wounded trust. Some of us find it hard to trust anyone because of the defenses we have built throughout our lives. Often we have deceived ourselves into believing we have no trust issues until our Heavenly Father allows the covers to be pulled back and we are exposed. I discovered that I had serious holes in my trust fabric when my marriage came apart. Had I lived in a condition of distrust in my intimate relationship for too long? Had I allowed my trust for my spouse to erode so much that it was only a scant veneer? Had

that erosion of trust actually affected my ability to trust my

Lord and Savior? Those questions plagued me as I struggled

to recover from the feelings of betrayal.

Over and over like a wounded animal, I had begun to

recoil from the tender wooing of my Savior's call to trust

him. Soon after the separation, during my prayer time,

the Lord shared tender promises that he loved me. He had

chosen me. He would protect me and never forsake me. All

these I gained from comforting passages in Isaiah.

But now thus saith the Lord that created thee, O Jacob And he that formed thee, O Israel. Fear not, for I have redeemed thee, I have called thee by thy name; thou art mine. When thou passest through the waters, I will be with thee, and through the rivers, they shall not overflow thee, when thou walkest through the fire thou shalt not be burned, neither shall the flame kindle upon thee.
Isaiah 43:1-2

*Remember ye not the former things, neither consider the
things of old.
Behold I will do a new thing now it shall spring forth;
shall ye not know it?
I will even make a way in the wilderness, and rivers in
the desert.*

Isaiah 43:18-19

I was afraid to fully trust God with my future and I had a

hard time not remembering the former things to prepare for

that which was new. I still wanted my husband even though

he had wounded me so often and so deeply. I think I felt

security in what I knew- a routine of normalcy peppered

with intensifying betrayal and pain. I was afraid to let go of

the past to chance an unconditional surrender to the Master

who held the unseen future of promise. In many ways, I was

much like the freed Hebrew slaves who murmured and com-

plained about longing for the leeks and melons of Egypt they

had eaten under the task master's whip while they steadily

ate the food of heaven without much appreciation. How

shameful and absurd to cry over Egypt who had enslaved

their lives and slaughtered their dreams. It was just as stupid for me to long to be back in a relationship that had nearly killed me for years and was painting an unhealthy marriage picture for our children.

Yes, the Lord constantly reminded me that he loved me, wanted me and would never abandon me. He said these words to me through the Scriptures:

> *For thy Maker is thine husband; the Lord of hosts is his name; and thy Redeemer the Holy One of Israel, the God of the whole earth shall he be called. For the Lord hath called thee as a woman forsaken and grieved in spirit, and a wife of youth, when thou wast refused, saith thy God. For a small moment have I forsaken thee; but with great mercies will I gather thee.*   Isaiah 54:5-7

God promised me he would care for me and be my covering when I was rejected by my husband. These words really registered in my heart one day when God gave me a visual picture. I remember sitting and praying in the family room that the children and I had recently redecorated to prepare our home for sale. As I sat alone on the sofa enjoying the warm sunbeams from the window on my skin, I fell into a deep trance. I saw a vision of a pond filled with dark, oily and muddy waters. Then I saw the hand of God reach down into the muddy waters and pull out a woman in a white gown. Strangely all the oil and mud slid off of the woman's skin and clothing and she emerged dazzling clean. The voice of the Lord said this is you my daughter, Cynthia. I have delivered you from a miry mess and I have allowed you to emerge clean by my hand. As I came to myself, I wept and praised God because it was true. He had delivered me from some bad situations of the past. As a young child he had brought me through years of sexual abuse at the hand of my paternal grandfather. Now he had brought me out of a marriage situation where my soul was being vexed by pornography, adultery and the continual erosion of my self-esteem. I had endured tearful and sleepless nights, arguments and fights, private and public humiliations. My body had suffered sickness and surgeries brought on by a venereal disease, continual stress, and broken rest. That's not to mention the mental confusion and anguish of loving a gifted and charming man who more and more often had taken on the characteristics of a possessed tormented and restless spirit. His distaste for the things of God and family life, the lies, insomnia, ungodly insatiable sexual desires, and the craving for a secret night life became more and more frightening. It was even more difficult to cover up. I should have been dead many times over, but God spared me and our children. God kept his promise to me to give me spirit-filled children who would turn the world upside down for Christ. Despite the things they witnessed and experienced in Life as preacher's kids their love for God is still strong and intact.

By his grace, my own faith in God is also stronger than ever. Jesus reminded me of all the things I had been through so I could stop glamorizing the past by only remembering the happy family times and the sense of security I felt as a wife. I wish I could say I received this message and never fell back into despair, but that would not even be close to the truth. No, for several months and even years, I struggled with trusting my Lord's ability to care for me and to help me keep my sanity. The mental anguish I experienced came from my own perceptions of success and my desire to be well spoken of by others. But Jesus said,

> *If any man will come after me, let him deny himself, and take up his cross daily, and follow me. For whosoever will save his life shall lose it, but whosoever will lose his life for my sake, the same shall save it.* Luke 9:23-24

I now have a clearer understanding of that scripture. I used to apply it to Christian martyrdom for the sake of the gospel, but now I understand it is a daily surrendering process of my will to that of the Lord's. So, like the disciples, I hear Jesus saying bring all you have to me for my use, my direction, for my glory—and watch me do a new thing in your life. I used to be fearful of failure and I dreaded this verse: **"But Jesus told him, anyone who lets himself be distracted from the work I plan for him is not fit for the** *kingdom of God*," Luke 9:62. But now I have the assurance that the Lord has broken the strong soul ties I had to the past, and I believe I shall fulfill the will of God for my life. Now, I can declare like the Apostle Paul said in Philippians 3:13-14: *Brethren, I count not myself to have apprehended; but this one thing I do, forgetting those things which are behind and reaching forth unto those things which are before, I press toward the mark for the prize of the high calling of God in Christ Jesus.*

The Lord has shown me many visions of healing, teaching and preaching the gospel throughout the world. My goal is to fulfill that call. I am determined to walk in freedom because too many years I have spent locked up in a prison of despair, self-hatred, shame, loneliness, guilt, fear and poverty. Christ came into my life a long time ago and saved me, but I still allowed my mind to keep me in prison. I refused to believe fully that God wanted the best for me. I had refused to grasp the words of my Lord who said: I know the thoughts that I think toward you, saith the Lord, thoughts of peace and not of evil to give you an expected end. Jeremiah 29:11. I've chosen to trust my future to his hands. The Lord, Jesus Christ is calling us to place all our concerns, crumbs of strength and mountains of fears in his hands through prayer.

The disciples had to trust the only little food they had gathered to the dependable hands of Jesus. We too must trust all of our resources to him for multiplication, direction and distribution. I prayed the following prayer to the Lord while going through a frustrating period without gainful employment. I was so fearful that I would not realize my purpose or would fail to fulfill my God designed purpose more than not having provision. Left to my own devices, I know I can make a royal mess of my life, so I knew I had better give my plans, hopes, efforts and faith to him and to him alone. In essence I brought my multitude of issues to him so he could take full control:

Lord,
I want a job. I want to do something meaningful that will bless people and further your will in the earth. I want your kingdom to come and your will to be done on earth the way it is done in heaven. Lord, I am helpless and feeble. I have had grandiose dreams and good intentions, but I lack strength to give birth, to consistently bring forth that which I believe you have given me. Often, I have derided myself and whipped myself mentally, but that process is to no avail. I still end up in the same location, lost. Dear Father, I blame no one else but me. I am sorry. I have barely struggled through the fast. My prayers have been pretty lousy and the reading of your Holy Word sporadic. I do long to please you, but my flesh seems to constantly to derail me. Lord! Have mercy on me a sinner! Blot out my transgressions and cleanse me of my sin. I loathe the iniquity in my heart because you deserve so much better than a worm like me. Please help me not to cause any more pain and loss. I want to be a blessing to others. Please, oh God, remember me!

God's Word answers the fears and questions in my life and yours, no matter what we face: a lack of job, sickness, depression, trouble with the children, difficulty with our spouses, problems concerning our aging parents, etc. The prophet Isaiah was used once again to reassure you and me that God is more than able and willing to come to our rescue.

Have you not known?
Have you not heard?
The Creator of the ends
of the earth,
The Everlasting God,
the Lord,
Neither faints nor is weary.

His understanding is
unsearchable.
Shall renew their strength;

They shall mount up with
wings like eagles,

He gives power to the weak,
And to those who have no might
He increases strength.

And the young men shall
utterly fall,
Even the youths shall faint
and be weary,
But those who wait on the
Lord
They shall run and not
be weary,
They shall walk and not faint.
Isaiah 40:28-31

As believers we can trust in the power and knowledge of the Heavenly Father, the Almighty God to give strength, know-how and motivation to achieve his will here on the earth. Each of us has been created for a divine purpose, and I believe it gives the Father delight when we turn to him for help both in the discovery and fulfillment of that purpose. Being plagued with a fallen nature, we spend an enormous amount of time trying to circumvent God in either determining or in carrying out our purpose. Since Adam and Eve, we have been determined to do things our way.

Unfortunately, Christians are not exempt from wandering down the self-sufficient, self-aggrandizement lane either. We want to do it on our own, do it our way and do it for our own glory far too often. Although we have been made a new creation in Christ, we still have to deal with our flesh and a mind that must be renewed. In order to avoid the daily temptation to ignore the Holy Spirit's guidance around these sinful pitfalls, we must remain sensitive to the Holy Spirit via prayer, continual immersion in and obedience to God's Word. It is tempting to assume your memory serves you well enough to remind you of the truths in Scripture without actually frequenting the pages of the Holy Bible, but don't be duped by the enemy. Nothing replaces the meditation on the written Word of God when it is available to be read or listened to. Jesus said, "...the words that I speak to you are spirit and they are life" (John 6:63). Consequently, as living creatures we need to feed on those things which will supply us with life. We don't need much encouragement to feed our physical bodies, judging by the increasing size of airplane and auditorium seats. Nevertheless, like a child who fights eating his vegetables we lock our spiritual lips and refuse to consistently partake of the scriptural nourishment so generously provided by our loving Savior. Some of us smart little kids have even ventured to become skillful in camouflaging our defiant lack of discipline to eat that which is good by perpetually stirring around in the same old spiritual peas in order to make it look like we are really absorbing the manna the Lord has provided. You know how we read a few verses a week without trying to apply their truths to the depths of our soul. At other times while engaged in conversation, we spout some spiritual platitudes we learned years ago when we still had a good appetite for the Word of God, hoping all the while that no one in our Christian circles finds out how spiritually undernourished we really are. Who are we trying to fool anyway? Certainly not God! We are missing the point. The Lord already knows us and loves us. He supplied us with the Word to strengthen, prepare, repair and renew us. Racking up "brownie points" in the eyes of men means absolutely nothing. Getting about the transforming business of renewing our minds through the meditation on the word of God, however, will profit our lives and others for all eternity.

History has countless examples of individual as well as collective values that are added to Life by one who spends ample quality time reading and following the Word of God. Famous scientist and inventor Dr. George Washington Carver, equipped with a strong faith in Jesus Christ, dedication to the study of God's Word and to the service of mankind, discovered hundreds of uses for the peanut, soybean, sweet potato and pecan. His inventions and improvements include such things as linoleum, mayonnaise, adhesives, axle grease, bleach, chili sauce, buttermilk, instant coffee, synthetic rubber, ink, shoe polish, metal polish, paper, talcum powder, wood stain, fuel briquettes, and other inventions we use every day. He lived by the words of Proverbs

3:5-6, "*Trust in the Lord with all thine heart. And lean not on your own understanding; in all thy ways acknowledge Him, and he shall direct thy paths.*" Fame, wealth and pride are not numbered among his prized possessions because, although he did garner fame, he took no pleasure in it. Rather, he sought to follow God and to help mankind by following the guidance of the Holy Spirit. He credited God with giving him insights into the profound discoveries he made, which continue to benefit mankind in this country, and around the world. Dr. Carver's legacy alone inspires me to seek the Lord to direct and order my steps by his Word. His life is a witness to the accuracy of God's promise in Romans 12:2: "And be not conformed to this world but be ye transformed by the renewing of your mind that you may prove what is that good and acceptable and perfect will of God."

Like Dr. Carver and others, great accomplishments began with faith to read and to believe the word of God, but those accomplishments blossomed through having enough love for God and others to put faith into action. I have been so guilty over these several years of being slow to do the last part. I could use the excuse of having an unhealthy fear of failure, but the very Word of God that covers and protects me also convicts me. Hasn't it been written that "I can do all things through Christ who strengthens me?" (Philippians 4:13). However, until the words that are visualized on the page become actualized in our belief system, we will not experience real transformation in our lives. Many of us spend ten, twenty, or thirty plus years agonizing over our shortcomings instead of pointedly meditating on the only power source that can elevate us from the pit of despair to the apex of victory. We overcome by faith, but "faith comes by hearing and hearing by the word of God" (Romans 10:17). For months, the Holy Spirit has been poking and prodding me to focus on the words in the twelfth chapter of Romans, but like a stubborn defiant child I refused to allow the transforming absorption of God's word to take effect in my spirit.

I became angry with God and began to doubt that he was even leading me to read these words time and time again. But now I get it. I had been continually asking him to tell me what I needed to study in His word so I could have faith to accomplish the work he had for me to do, namely to write about some lessons learned through God's grace. Finally, I discovered that he was showing me the answer all along. He was telling me that if I would meditate on dedicating my body to him as a living sacrifice and to focus on being changed by making my mind new through his Word, I would actually "prove" (accomplish) his "perfect" (complete) will for my life. I had previously looked up scriptures about writing, but they addressed how to write and also what to write. My particular problem was having the faith to rid myself of negative thinking about succeeding. I needed to believe that I wasn't a broken mess and I could accomplish anything God assigned my hands to do. Like a computer virus can eventually affect all your programs and cause the computer to become inoperable, "stinking thinking" can make your faith inoperable. If a person continues to allow negative thoughts like, "I know God can do anything, but I don't know if he can use me because I am a real mess" or "Leave it to me and I'll mess up every time" to permeate and remain in her spirit she will become spiritually stalled like a car filled with bad gasoline. Holding onto negative mindsets, sap your joy and your strength. It will also blind you to the possibilities God has for your life. Until I decided to change my self-talk and my personal prayers, I stayed stuck in a deep rut. So instead I thought and prayed:

God has a purpose for me. My job is to discover what that purpose is and then to commit my life to Him and the fulfillment of that purpose. Today, I have decided to put aside my fears, my pride, and my laziness to yield my body for the glory of God. Lord, I don't know how all this will come about, but if you'll show me how I will press on by faith. Help me please, Lord. I don't want to be a cripple in my mind anymore. No matter what has happened in my past, I have no excuse to be a coward or to waste all the resources You have given me. Instead of letting my light shine inside, which is not blessing anyone, I will seek to use what I have to help someone else. I remember when I struggled with Chemistry during my first semester of college. At that time, I had let my fear of failure and my feelings of incompetence paralyze me, but a simple visit to the professor encouraged me to believe I could do it. To my amazement, I became one the top students in class the very next semester. I have as much as some and more than others. I have been blessed with wonderful children, family and friends. I have a home of my own and transportation simply because my loving heavenly Father desired to bless me with the desires of my heart besides my daily needs. I have not always been grateful, however. On the contrary, I have often experienced depression, self- pity, and ungratefully bad attitudes. Yes, I really did experience some rejection and abuse in the past, but I also was greatly loved and given more favor than I ever deserved. My mother, grandparents, aunts, uncles, sisters, brother and cousins have shown me much love and support. I am so grateful for my loving children and their spouses. I am really sorry for struggling so long with you, Lord. Please forgive me. Give me another chance, Lord to change and to humble myself for use. Thank you for giving your life as a ransom for my sinful soul. Thank you for setting me free, Jesus.

I recently made a discovery that made me both happy and embarrassed at the same time. Have you ever had that happen to you? That was the second time in little over a month I'd had this experience. I was beginning to think maybe God was trying to teach me something. The first time this phenomenon occurred, I had (after much prompting from the Lord to invest in myself by buying a new computer) just purchased my first laptop computer. I was excited because it was shiny, new, expensive, portable and usable. My old desktop had been in storage for over four years since my divorce and for some reason I thought I could just unpack it, connect it to my internet system, install a new printer and begin typing away. Wrong! To my amazement, I discovered the connections didn't fit and the old computer's processor was too slow to handle the speed and amount information sent through the new internet system. I had to change my hardware before I could even begin to function.

Frequently, we hold on to things of the past that have lost their usefulness and when we try to function in the Present we are stopped dead in our tracks. We try to hold on to old mindsets, old hurts and disappointments while trying to function in a new day that God has given us and we continue to hit snags and freeze up like my old computer. Jesus said we cannot put new wine into old wineskins or the bottles will burst and all the good new wine will spill out. (Matthew 9:17)

After my new laptop arrived, I was eager to pop in the installation CD for the Internet service. Because I was accustomed to my former desktop computer's CD Rom, which operated by partially inserting a disc into a slot and the machine would grasp it and suck it in, I was a little challenged when I tried to gently press the diskette onto this new drive. At first glance it seemed to not fit and immediately I thought I had a defective machine. So I said to myself, "I've charged all this money and the thing doesn't even work!" You can bet I got on the phone with the company right away and informed them my CD/DVD driver was defective. (I was trying to sound like I knew what I was talking about). The representative was very courteous and she asked me if I was sure? I told her I was quite sure. The little hole in the middle of the disc was smaller than the spigot it had to fit on.

Of course, I was going by what it looked like to the naked eye. I didn't dare try to press it on because it might break. She asked me if I had any other CDs or DVDs. I rushed over to my TV cabinet taking out one of the few movies I owned and again tried laying a disc on top of the spigot while applying little or no pressure. I even tried to close the thing up hoping it would fall into place but it slid out of place. The representative said she had never heard of such a defect, but agreed to rush me a new driver with instructions on how to install it. I thanked her but was disappointed that I couldn't install my new software. I took my new laptop over to my daughter and son-in-law's and related my story to them. He listened intently without displaying any disbelief and then quietly picked up one of his own CDs and popped it onto the spigot. I stood there aghast! He showed me how some of the little parts retracted to accommodate the size of the disk as he applied a small amount of pressure. My fear of breaking my new computer had hindered me from having the fun and full use of it for several days. How foolish.

Apparently, I was still not getting the message God was trying to show me because not long afterward, I discovered my favorite set of sheets that were folded on the top shelf of my closet actually fit my oversized mattress. I had purchased them more than a year earlier. At the time, the label didn't indicate extra deep pockets to accommodate my new mattress, so I thought they wouldn't fit. I hadn't gotten rid of the sheets yet because they matched my comforter set and I couldn't bring myself to part with them. To think that I had been washing two sets of sheets to death because I thought I didn't have a third set that fit. Another case of **False** **E**xpectations **A**ppearing **R**eal (**F.E.A.R.**) had restricted and delayed my enjoyment of the things God had already provided for me.

You may think this is humorous and maybe even a little silly, but God correlated these events in my life with the

Scriptures to teach me some truths. I had just spent several years going through hurts, disappointments and financial difficulties. All through those years I kept looking for the silver lining in the situation experiencing great highs and lows in my Christian walk. Somewhere along the journey, however, I had begun to believe the devil's trash talk. I became afraid to trust God, my Heavenly Father to work out things for my best. Instead of my faith ruling my mind I had begun to let an emotion, fear, direct my thinking. Whenever fear is allowed to "ride shotgun" over your life, you cannot experience the fullness of joy, peace and provisions that God has for you. It's not that the Lord is holding them back from you. No, your own mind limits you. Your thoughts convince you that you will fail before you try. You believe that things won't come together and if anybody can mess things up, you can. Whenever thoughts like these dominate your thinking, the flesh and fear are operating in your life and not faith. Faith expects the good things that God has promised and it opens your heart to receive them. Right before I decided to try the

sheet set on the bed with the intention of seeing if it would

fit before I gave them away, I had read in the following

Scriptures in my devotion time:

*According as his divine power hath given unto us all
things that pertain unto life and godliness, through the
knowledge of him that hath called us to glory and virtue.*
II Peter 1:3

and

*[God] Who hath saved us, and called us with an holy
calling, not according to our own works, but according
to his own purpose and grace, which was given us in
Christ Jesus before the world began,* *II Timothy 1:9*

The scriptures seemed to leap off the page with new hope

and inspiration. These words promised a limitless future of

success in Christ which was already pre-arranged before

the world was created. The scripture revealed that when I

became a believer in Christ, I gained access to the knowledge of my purpose and the enabling grace to fulfill that purpose during my lifetime.

When I first became a Christian at fourteen, I believed I could do just about anything through Christ. God did some absolutely miraculous things in my life, but I also spent a lot of time comparing myself to others and wishing I could be a better Christian like my friend, Cheryl. I often tried to bury or hide those feelings of inadequacy and doubt. However, when the trials and tests of life began to beat down on me, they increasingly manifested areas of insecurity. On the surface I believed God's Word but deep inside I felt like it depended a lot on my ability to do things the right way. I thought if I prayed right, worked hard enough, knew enough scripture, and to the best of my ability avoided sinning against God and my fellow man, God would come through for me every time. I didn't realize that even though I believed Jesus loved me and died for my sin, I felt like the things I did or didn't do right affected that love. The word of God lets us know that we love God because he first loved us. He loved us with a perfect unconditional love that prompted him to send his very best—his Son—to deliver us from the prison of sin and death. Trusting in that perfect love liberates us from the bondage of fear of falling or failing. The verses mentioned earlier in II Timothy and II Peter guarantee our victory in Christ, not in self. In II Peter 1:3, the Word of God promises that we are given every single thing we need to live a godly victorious life when we believe, are born again and therefore come into covenant with Jesus Christ. In II Timothy 1:9, we see that we were called and chosen by God. It really wasn't our idea, so we have no need to worry about rejection if we don't measure up to the sometimes unrealistic goals we set for ourselves. This same verse reassures us that we were given a specific purpose on earth by God himself, so there is a reason we are here on earth and a reason why our gifts are needed in the body of Christ. Just knowing these facts is enough to shout about, but having a determination to really know Christ and to glorify him by completing his destined work for our hands gives real fulfillment. As I learned from my experience with the computer disc, to get results we must press ourselves to operate in a renewed mindset. We must learn to depend on Christ's sufficiency and not our own. Often it is not comfortable at first, and it appears that you are not cut out for that type of thinking, but the Holy Spirit wants you and I to press in and see we won't break. Once we learn to truly trust Him, a world of truth, peace and blessing will unfold to us.

Until now we have spent a lot of time discussing how to trust God for everything we need in life. Our next topic will deal with the role of obedience in a person's life.

Let Jesus Command
Your Multitude

Chapter 5

*And He commanded them to make all sit down by com-
panies upon the green grass. And they sat down in ranks,
by hundreds and fifties. Mark 6:39-40*

He, Jesus, commanded the disciples to make everyone sit down in orderly groups of fifties and hundreds on the green grass. It is interesting that two of the gospel writers chose the word "commanded" to denote the manner in which Jesus gave instructions regarding the multitude of people to be served. Until now we have spent a lot of time talking about trust. Specifically, we have discussed trusting God for everything we need in life. We have talked about this trust being born out of a love relationship between us and a heavenly Father who has lovingly shown us grace and mercy. In the previous verses the disciples were requested to give the food and their trust to the Master for his use. Immediately following that request comes a detailed command requiring obedient action. Why is that? Real trust gives way to obedience. The word "command" means to order, direct or to put upon one as a duty. How could Jesus, who is so compassionate, meek, loving and trustworthy turn around and begin to demand or command the disciples and this multitude? The answer is simply because he has a right to. Jesus explained obedience as being the outward sign of an inward commitment:

"If you love me, keep my commandments," John 14:15.

&

He that hath my commandments, and keepeth them, he it is that loveth me and he that loveth me shall be loved of my Father and I will love him, and will manifest myself to him.
John 14:21

I think the Master made it very clear that the sign of real love and relationship is the willingness and action of obedience to his instructions. Because we say that we trust in God and we know that he loves us, then it follows that if we love him in return we should put action behind our words and obey him. Earlier I made a statement that may puzzle some people: God has a right to command us or give us direction. The Scriptures tell us that Christ made us and everything in this earth. They also reveal that we were made for his purposes and therefore he has the place of supreme authority:

For by him all things were created: things in heaven and on earth,

> *visible and invisible, whether thrones or powers or rulers or authorities; all things were created by him and for him. He is before all things, and in him all things hold together. And he is the head of the body, the church; he is the beginning and the firstborn from the dead, so that in everything he might have the supremacy. Colossians 1:16-18 NIV*

The Bible further tells us that obedience is not only a sign of our love relationship, but it is also the way to abide in that love relationship. Jesus went so far as to explain that we have been invited into the same relationship he has with his Father: *If ye keep my commandments, ye shall abide in my love; even as I have kept my Father's commandments, and abide in his love.* John 15:10. So obedience is the other part of trust, which is to be equally embraced.

Jesus was talking to twelve men who left everything to follow him. He had walked, slept and eaten with these men for over a year and they had carefully watched his every move. Jesus had poured himself into them, and freely imparted wisdom to them by word and demonstration. Although they did not fully grasp the knowledge of who he was, they knew enough to obey his commands without question because he had proven time and again that he knew what he was doing. They had observed as he commanded the servants of the wedding to fill the water pots with water, which miraculously became exquisite wine. They had watched as he commanded the blind man to go and wash in the pool and when he returned he could see. They listened as he commanded the lepers to go show themselves to the priest and saw new skin cells form where once rotting flesh clung. These twelve men had learned to trust Jesus enough to obey. They knew that he did what he said and he fulfilled what he promised. So, without hesitation, they followed his instructions.

In the text Jesus gave the disciples clear instructions as to how to position the multitude to receive their meal. He told them to put the people in groups of fifties and hundreds. I think this instruction had a two-fold purpose. He made the groups manageable and countable. God doesn't put us in situations that we can't bear, and he always sets it up so we can remember and recount the details of our blessings. The Lord always sets us up to win. Even when we face what seems like an insurmountable multitude of problems, when we give control to Christ and follow the leading of the Holy Spirit, he will tell us how to put things in order. The Holy Spirit will actually give step by step instructions.

I remember when God challenged me to obey him by placing my home for sale. At the time, my ex-husband and I were separated, but my children and I still lived in the home. In November the previous year, the Lord had told me to sell my house and move to Connecticut, but I had been dragging my feet. Financially, it was a struggle holding on to it and keeping up the utility payments, but it represented security and safety. In my eyes, because my husband was gone, my home represented a hope that our lives would one day return to normalcy again. I had convinced myself that I would obey God, but I was delaying, hoping things would come together again. Delayed obedience of course is disobedience. So one morning as I sat in the living room having my quiet time, I heard the Lord ask me: "Cynthia, do you love me more than these?" I asked him, "these what?" He answered "These four walls and all your stuff you are so attached to." I told him

I loved him more than my house and my possessions. He commanded me sternly then to sell the house, give away my accumulated stuff and move to Connecticut. At that moment, the fear of God entered my heart and I knew I could not dilly dally any longer. I asked him to show me what to do and I would obey beginning that morning. He led me to call the very same real estate office my husband had previously worked in and to ask a realtor to come over and tell me what needed to be done to prepare the house for sale. Let me tell you I was filled with questions and fear about the unknown. What if my husband tried to block the sale? He was still half owner of the house although he wasn't living with us. What if there were major things that needed to be done which I couldn't do and couldn't afford to pay anyone to do? But the Holy Spirit reassured me it would work out fine. He told me to get a notepad ready so when the realtor came I could just take notes of the things I needed to do. When I called the real estate office, the person was very nice and agreed to do a walk through the next day. To my surprise it wasn't

as painful as I thought. She told me what needed to be done

such as removing clutter, painting, spackling, changing the

kitchen flooring, repairing a banister etc. I had always relied

upon my husband for reassurance to tackle big jobs, so I felt

a bit overwhelmed and unskilled to face the challenge. As

I prayed about the things on the list the Lord directed me

to read the book of Nehemiah. For the first time, I really

paid attention to how the people in the city were instructed

to repair the wall. I noticed that each person repaired the

part of the wall nearest to them and everyone worked on the

common areas. In essence, the Lord showed me that this was

the way we should tackle the work to be done in the house.

So we sat down as a family and discussed what needed to be

done based on the realtor's recommendations. We looked at

all the rooms and figured out specific plans. Then we began

to tackle the areas according to the time table we set up.

Each of us needed to work on our own rooms to remove any

clutter and then as needed we helped each other to repaint the rooms in neutral colors. Amazingly, we had a lot of fun as we all worked on the common areas together. That's what I mean by saying God will direct you to put your problems in manageable segments.

I had to call my husband and let him know I wanted to put the house on the market. He agreed, but said he didn't like the realtor I had chosen. He said he wanted to choose the realtor. His request threw me into a tailspin again. You see I felt I couldn't trust him to keep our family's best interest at heart. Besides being involved in an affair, he had previously conspired with the same woman to cancel my plane ticket for a trip we had planned to Israel with our church.

This person was a fairly new member of the church, who had come in spreading her money around and wowing my husband with her business know-how. She told us about a reasonably priced tour package that would allow many our members to go to the Holy Lands and assured us she had coordinated and taken several trips like this before. As a dutiful wife, I had orchestrated getting the flyers made, facilitating the meetings and getting people from church all excited to go. We had scheduled the plane tickets, people had paid their monies and everything, but shortly before the planned trip departure date, everything blew up. Her daughter sent a letter to the deacons of the church disclosing his scandalous behavior, the same day I had confronted him about my suspicions that he was having an affair with her. I couldn't see how we could possibly go on this trip together after the turn of events. In his presence, I called the travel agent from his church office to find out possible options for canceling the trip, but that's when I found out that my ticket had been canceled months earlier. When confronted my husband said he didn't know anything about my ticket being canceled by the woman, but he didn't defend me so obviously he was aware of the plan. As it turned out everyone went on the trip, but me.

After experiencing my husband's betrayal, I figured he merely wanted to get possession of my interest in the house and to leave me destitute. I felt very vulnerable and unprepared to protect myself in dealing with my husband who was now aligned with this wealthy, shrewd woman. I prayed and cried about my fears and the Lord reassured me he would work everything out for my good. He said for me to agree to let my husband choose the realtor. To my surprise, I gained favor with the realtor he chose, and she even offered to donate some of her proceeds from the sale to our church. God told me exactly how much to ask for the house and when to expect it to sell. The realtor thought I should put it on the market for a slightly higher amount, but as God promised it sold for the original amount one month after it was listed. God had blessed me to see his hand at work. My faith grew and the children and I had a memorable experience restoring our home. It looked so good by the time it was put on the market I almost wanted to buy it myself. Following

God's step-by-step instructions blessed me to come out on top. I split the proceeds of the house with my husband and gave him possession of the better car. So now I had a fresh future, debt free. I learned like the disciple's that the Lord always knows what he is doing and he does it right. I guess that's why the disciples usually responded to him so quickly.

I was always fascinated by the King James rendition of the way the disciples responded to Jesus' commands. I remember reading that Jesus said, "Come after me and I will make you to become fishers of men" (Mark 1:17) and then the bible said "And straightway they forsook their nets, and followed him." (Mark 1:18). It seemed that when the Lord gave a command, it was immediately followed by his disciples, the blind, the lame and even the dead. There was never much of a debate, but simple obedience led to miraculous benefits and results. I was so impressed, I told the Lord, "Lord, I want to be your straightway girl!" I meant that I wanted to be a person that he could instruct and count on to obey at all times.

Those words were easier to say than to do, I discovered. Lip service is easy. It's much easier than real obedient service. I said those words to God in prayer shortly after I answered my call to serve the Lord in ministry, but when God began to shape me by challenging my real motives and desires, I found I too frequently rebelled. I don't know if you have ever struggled with the issue of rebellion, but I have. I rebelled through making excuses. I rebelled by procrastination. I rebelled by filibustering or asking questions for clarification over and over. I didn't like what I saw, but God showed me what was really in my heart.

Much of the time when God asked me to do something that made sense to me, I didn't squawk and I quickly did it. For instance, when God led me to bring a homeless woman into my home and give her a hot meal instead of giving her money to support her habit, I felt glad to do it. But when the

Spirit of God led me to go on a 21-day fast in preparation for a ministry conference, I really balked and procrastinated for several days. I wanted confirmation a few times to ensure this was really God. After all, I do like to eat and to me 21 days was a bit extreme. I had no idea, of course, the magnitude at which God was going to manifest himself to me within the next few weeks or how much he would later use me through yielding in obedience to his instruction. During that same preparation period, God had also instructed some of his other children in Louisiana to go on a 21-day fast in preparation for the conference. I was unaware of their fast and they were unaware of mine until shortly before the conference. Once I learned about their fast, it confirmed what God had required me to do. That is the beauty of the way God does things. We feel all alone at times, but he is always at work behind the scenes.

Sometimes you can receive confirmation from God through Scripture or a sermon being preached. Other times

God may have another believer to confirm his words to you through their words or the fact that they are going through the same thing. I used to marvel at the number of times I would hear a sermon from my pastor on Sunday morning only to get in the car and turn on my radio to hear the same sermon being preached by another preacher. When I would call my mom and other family members in another city, I often heard their pastor had preached the same sermon using the same scripture text. I thought that was so amazing. Later, I began to understand that the messages were coming from the same person, God- the Holy Spirit, so it made perfect sense. God, the Father is orchestrating the lives of his children and he is the one who determines what his children need to know through the Spirit. So of course, we would hear the same message, with perhaps a slight variation, going forth in different areas at the same time. I don't know about you, but that's encouraging news. Something as simple as these types of confirmations, reassure me that I am in the safe hands of someone bigger than myself. He has an infallible plan already mapped out for me and the rest of his children. Hallelujah! Why shouldn't we want to follow and obey every command God gives us?

In Romans 8:28, we are promised that in the final analysis we win: *"And we know that all things work together for good to them that love God and are the called according to his purpose"*. Understand the scripture doesn't say all things feel good or are good, but rather that all of them together will work out for our good. For example, it wasn't good when that semi-truck rear ended my little compact car, but along with recuperation time, it worked together to bring me into focus about what God had actually called me to do in my life. I learned that I must contend for the faith during a time when society is pushing for compromise and all out rejection of the gospel of Jesus Christ.

Such a close brush with death made me remember my own frailty and mortality. It made me realize how important it is to stay focused on glorifying Christ with all the days I have upon this earth. Sure I loved my Savior and his people. I loved going to church and also preaching his Gospel, but the urgency for reaching the Lost had begun to lull into complacency.

I believe obedience must be fueled with passion or else we will give up when the going gets tough. When our Savior, who was fully God and fully man incarnate, faced the agonizing torture of the cross he pressed onward. I am sure that if he had not possessed a passionate love for the Father and for us, he would not have willingly endured such agony. He had many opportunities to draw back and willfully disobey his Father, but he didn't. Instead he brought his flesh and emotions under subjection through prayer and worship. He sought God the Father frequently in open and honest prayer for strength and direction.

We find examples of this throughout Scripture. In particular, Jesus' diligent prayer life is referenced in the first chapter of the book of Mark: *And in the morning, rising up a great while before day, he went out and departed into a solitary place and there prayed.* Mark 1:35. Jesus carefully followed his instructions daily and to the letter. He was careful to tell onlookers the reason why he did what he did. He gave all the glory to the Father and in turn the Father glorified him. Jesus stayed focused even when family and friends thought he was crazy and tried to pull him away from obediently following his purpose. Listen to what happened to Jesus as he and his disciples ministered to a crowd of people who showed up unannounced at meal time: *"And when those who belonged to Him (His kinsmen) heard it, they went out to take Him by force, for they kept saying, he is out of his mind. (beside Himself, deranged)."* Mark 3:21 AMP.

Obedience is definitely not without a cost to the individual and those who care about them. As I have tried to follow Christ in obedience, I have encountered difficulties and tests that were also shared by my family and friends. Some could not understand what God was doing with me.

When I walked away from a career in banking where I was garnering awards, etc., it affected our household budget, and people began to talk. I had wrestled for years with God's call and discussed God's instruction for me to leave my position at work with my husband before making the step. We both agreed; nevertheless, there was a cost involved. When God commands us to surrender to his will there is a definite sifting of motives and a challenging of faith that takes place. Often you may feel alone and pressured to the breaking point, but God is there the whole time watching over you, molding you and working on your behalf. Many days and nights I was unsure that I was correctly following God's leading when he'd challenge me to obey in an area out of my comfort zone. I could only find solace and direction through his Word and pleading prayers like the one below:

Are you leading me, O Lord or am I delusional? I know I have heard in my mind and in my spirit, "write the book!", but why is it so difficult? I sometimes feel like I am losing my mind. You have blessed me with this beau-

tiful town home. You brought me through a serious car accident with a semi truck and then I get a revelation to leave my job. It doesn't make sense to a lot of people, but my mom believes in me. My kids are cheering me on to write, but the problem is me. I keep getting stuck in my mind. Sometimes it seems I am afraid of success and I would rather worry about the 'what- ifs'. Please help me Father. Your word says you will never leave me nor forsake me. You say that you are a very present help in the time of trouble and you are, but why do I have to travel this way? My mom is a survivor and go-getter. She takes a practical look at stuff and gets it done. I think, I dream but I have trouble formulating what to do and how to do it. Sure I can usually support a vision, but do I have it in me to birth a vision and work it in prayer and action until it materializes. I think that takes great faith. Maybe my faith hasn't been exercised that much yet. If it has, I don't see it. I have believed you for big things that develop quickly, but something that takes a long hard road I don't think I have ever had to endure before. Lord, I don't mind looking like a fool for a while when I know I am obeying what you want, because I know you will bring me through victoriously. I just am not sure I am on the right path now. Please confirm it for me and show me the way through this.

Every time I earnestly poured out my heart to God admitting my shortcomings and my fears, he lifted me up and gave me encouragement to persevere. Most times he would even clarify the situation for me as well. Sometimes there is no easy answer or quick fix and the only way accomplish what the Lord is requiring is sincere, dedicated faithfulness and obedience. Today many are being misled to believe everything works with a quick fix and no real labor. If that were true, we would miss out on the development God is working through us. Do not grieve the Holy Spirit by refusing to obey his promptings because of timidity, fear, disinterest or rebellion. Disobedience in these ways grieves the Holy Spirit because he has been sent to believers to guide us into all truth, and he is only speaking the things that he hears from the Father. When we choose to willfully and pridefully follow our own course of action rather than follow the leading of the Holy Spirit, we are in effect saying we feel our judgment is better than that of God. The Lord will not lead us in a path that is contrary to his word, nor will he lead us in a path that is not for our ultimate good.

Jesus modeled for us the attitude and response that should be given by every believer as God directs his steps.

Most people give attention to Christ's obedience displayed in the Garden of Gethsemane when facing crucifixion he said, "...*Father, if thou be willing, remove this cup from me: nevertheless not my will, but thine, be done.*" (Luke 22:42). But that statement was actually indicative of his entire life-style. Anyone who is familiar with the life of Jesus as he walked throughout Palestine for 33 and a half years, knows that his was a consistent life of obedience to the Father. He only spoke the words that he heard from the Father. He only did what he saw his father do and he did nothing of himself, (John 5:19; John 12:49 and John 8:28).

Isn't it interesting? Jesus hasn't asked us to do anything more than he has done. He consistently obeyed his Father even when it meant torture and ultimately crucifixion as seen in these verses:

And being found in fashion as a man, he humbled himself, and became obedient unto death, even the death of the cross.   *Philippians 2:8*

Though he were a Son, yet learned he obedience by the things which he suffered.   *Hebrews 5:8.*

So Jesus has asked us to be obedient to his words as well in the same way that he obeyed God the Father. Jesus indicated that the love relationship, which bears the fruit of obedience isn't a one-sided commitment. At first, I hadn't really thought much about the fact that there is a relationship between the promises contained in John 14:14 and the condition or request which is juxtaposed to it in the very next verse. But Jesus first promises his disciples that if they asked anything in His Name, he will do it. Then in almost the same breath, he says, "If you love me keep my commandments." That is the challenge that faces each of us daily.

Although absolute obedience is my heart's desire, I realize I am still a work in progress. Sometimes I find myself second guessing the instructions from the Lord because they don't seem to make sense according to the wisdom of the world. Other times I just don't want to do what I am told because of stubbornness. For example when God told me to pray daily for the welfare of my ex-husband and his wife, I felt like it didn't make sense and like it was an unfair request. I didn't know this was the method God used to deliver me from the bondage of un-forgiveness and bitterness. I did not begin to see and understand the plan of God until after I obeyed. This wasn't easy for me by any means because, like most I wanted to know what God was going to do before my flesh wanted to agree to it. I felt like a little child being asked to follow the leader's commands no matter what I was told to do. Remember God is not asking us to understand, but he does give us commands with the expectation of obedience. Disobedience leads to pain, disappointment and a lack of peace, but obedience to God's Word always leads to a far greater blessing.

Hallelujah! That's good news to my heart and to my ears. I have grown tired of feeling like the victim and the underdog. I am also glad that Jesus has commanded me to take authority over my multitude of fears and doubts. In 2 Corinthians 10:4, he says that we are to cast down vain imaginations and every high thing that exalts itself against the knowledge of God and then bring every thought unto the obedience of Christ. In other words, command the multitudes coming against your mind to get up under the authority of the Word of God. The disciples may have been timid to say everybody group up into groups of fifty. That's it! No more people in this group. You go over to that group. But like a young child who is sent out to get their older brother says with courage, "mommy or daddy says it is time to come in for dinner", the disciples were not acting in their own authority, but that of the Master.

Likewise, when we look at all the self-condemning feelings and thoughts about why we don't deserve to have the best, we can boldly say, "Jesus said all my sins, failures and mistakes are under his blood". He paid the price so I could be whole, so I could be well, and so I could have joy.

My job is to receive it and to believe it. By gaining control over my thought life, the Lord has positioned me to possess my Promised Land. Christ has promised so much to us as believers, but so many of us are living far beneath our privilege. We are living in the slave quarters when Christ has paid for and given us the mansion.

In Genesis 1:26 God created man and woman and he gave them authority and dominion over all the earth. When Satan convinced us to sin against our Heavenly Father, we gave that authority to Satan and we sold ourselves into slavery. Jesus gave his body and his life to pay the ransom for our liberty and when he arose he also announced that he had the keys and all power over heaven and earth in his hands. By trusting in him as our Lord and Savior, we have been set free with a complete pardon. Instead of a simple change of clothes and a probation officer, we have been given everything that pertains to life and godliness in Christ Jesus. In him our dominion has been restored and we are free to mani-

fest God's Kingdom rule here on planet earth.

God Giveth Grace To The Humble – Sit Down!

Chapter 6

*And Jesus said, "Make the men sit down." Now there was much grass in the place...*Mark 6:42

Can't you see this massive crowd gathered with many needs and desires? People who were tired of the disappointments of life were there. People who were young, full of strength, vitality and idealism were there. The suspicious, but curious aging were there waiting to hear what this young Rabbi, Jesus, had to say. Thrill seekers who needed healing and deliverance were there. People from all the different social ranks: priests, lawyers, doctors, dads, beggars, fishermen, carpenters, brick layers, tax collectors, little wide-eyed boys, seditionists (militant social changers), thieves, robbers, and others had all gathered to see the healing miracles he would perform. I have purposely left out the various types of women from the list of who was in the crowd, but they were definitely there. We will talk about them a little later.

These, like many of us, had grown accustomed to jostling for recognition, position and power in the workplace and even in the family. Like many of us they were accustomed to trying to make things happen for themselves. I can almost see the people in the crowd pushing and shoving as they tried to get in position to be noticed and blessed by Jesus. In our society, we have grown up on a diet of beliefs like "the early bird catches the worm", "it's the survival of the fittest", "it's a dog eat dog world" and "you'd better always look out for number one". These concepts were probably not foreign to the people living when Jesus walked the dusty roads of Palestine either.

In the time of this scene and still in most of the world today, men dominated the positions of leadership in government and in the workforce. During the time of the feeding of the five thousand, men were the only ones who sat at the city gates to discuss the affairs of state. In the Middle Eastern culture, being a male and especially an adult male of forty years or more was a position of entitlement and authority. When you became a man you learned to carry and to think about yourself differently. The Jewish brethren had boasted of a particular pride in their heritage of being the seed of Abraham. They had suffered disrespect and oppression for years under the tyranny of the Romans, but out there standing amongst their Jewish brethren, Jesus and the disciples, humility was probably the furthest thing from their minds. The fact that the young Rabbi Jesus wasn't even forty yet made his counsel and authority questionable among the elders. So, the indirect command from the mouth of one of his disciples may have really challenged the pride of every Jewish man in attendance that day. The disciple shouted "Sit down!" "Jesus said, sit down!" People rarely like being told what to do. Even though I am a woman, humble submission was one of the hardest lessons for me to learn as well. But didn't God say in James 4:6 that he "resists the proud, but gives grace to the humble"?

If I had been in that crowd and heard those words, I know of a time when I would have at least thought, "Sit down on the ground, for what?" But Jesus didn't offer a reason, he just said sit down. Perhaps as a carryover from my years of surviving sexual abuse as a child and struggling with feelings of rejection throughout many years of my life, I had learned to cling to pride and silent stubbornness for dear life. Such an attitude makes it hard for anyone to trust and not to be suspicious of someone who simply wants to render an act of kindness. But when Jesus told the people to sit down here, he meant: humble yourself, obey his word and trust him.

I wrestled with these very words for several years after answering God's call for me to preach. I was accustomed to doing things my way. On the outside, I may have appeared somewhat humble and even a bit docile at times, but to God who could really see my heart, I had a stubborn will akin to that of a wild bronco. When he'd tell me something to do, I wanted to know why and for how long? What's in it for me? What are others going to think? That sounds terrible doesn't it? But it's true nonetheless. But I learned the truth that, as the psalmist David wrote in the 23rd Psalm, "the Lord is my shepherd and I shall not want; he maketh me to lie down in green pastures…"

The five thousand who came to hear Jesus were in fact standing in a deserted place, but it was a pasture all the same. How do I know that? Because the scripture points out that there was much grass in the place. There was a lot of grass to cushion them as they sat. So Jesus wasn't trying to hurt them, but instead he was prompting them to take a load off of their feet and to get into the position to receive. We don't know how long it took the disciples to get all the men seated. We don't know if they had to hear complaints about joint stiffness, messing up their good clothes, and other complaints, but the disciples made them sit down. The scriptures say, "so the men sat down, in number about five thousand..."

Like these men, God wants us to come to a place of trusting obedience to follow his instructions because we know and love him. He wants us to know his character, that he is "good" through and through, and to know that he only wants to replenish the dry parched and starving places of our souls. But in order to fully receive, we must humble ourselves and sit down. We must put aside our own pride and self-sufficiency and recline, rest upon him.

One translation of this verse reads, "Jesus said make all the people recline (sit down)." In the Middle Eastern culture, reclining was the traditional position of eating. While eating, people reclined partially stretched out on their side and propped on one elbow perhaps so the food could properly digest. I also like this translation of the verse because it said make 'all' the people sit down, alluding to the fact that there were more than just men folk in the crowd. Yes, women and children were also there. Perhaps, there were married and unmarried women present. Widows, virgins, servant girls, prostitutes and maybe even women of prominence were there. Just because I spent a considerable amount of time detailing the men's issues with pride, don't think for a moment that there weren't many Martha's in the group.

You may recall Luke's account of the sisters Mary and Martha in Luke 10:38-42. Mary was the sister who sat at Jesus' feet when he came by and relished every word that dropped from his mouth. While Martha consumed with her own agenda, was quite frustrated and worn out from trying to make her home, the meal and the ambience measure up to the Hebrew's "Redbook" of etiquette. She wasn't happy because things weren't like she wanted and in her opinion that lazy Mary wasn't doing her fair share by sitting up under Jesus and listening to him teach like the men folk did. Martha probably thought to herself, "Who does Mary think she is? Remember, how Martha got up her nerve after having fumed to herself long enough to tell the Master about that lazy girl, Mary. However instead of being commended, Martha was gently reprimanded that she herself was too weighed down with worrying and wrong thinking. Jesus said she should have chosen the better part to seek him above everything else as Mary did. That was one of the first passages God began to use to deal with my heart when I began this ministry journey. And I hated it.

I didn't want to admit that I was like Martha. I was always trying to be a people pleaser. Rarely was there an uninterrupted moment of thought when I wasn't worried about what I should be doing according to other's opinion of me. I would worry about what was the right thing to wear, am I a good enough wife, or a good enough mom. It was a shame, but even in my efforts to really please my houseguests I would neglect them. On one occasion I remember my guests pulled me aside and reminded me that they wanted to spend time with me and not just eat food while catching glimpses of me coming to and from the kitchen like a slave girl.

I can imagine that although some of these women came out for the sole purpose of listening to Jesus, their attention may have also been distracted with many cares. Others may have reluctantly, but dutifully come along with their husbands and/or kids. More than likely several were getting very concerned about the lateness of the hour. They wanted to get back home to put some food on the table. Possibly these women thought, "Somebody has to keep a level head and not be caught up with all this idealistic thinking." Come on. Let's be real. Yes, we women struggle with our own issues of pride just like the men! They too had to be made to sit down – to humble themselves to receive from the Master.

I can readily identify with my sisters because although I really loved the Lord and prided myself in thinking I was a Mary deep down inside, I knew I was also weighed down with divided allegiance. I was worried about pleasing my husband, being super mom in the eyes of my kids, intelligent, productive and wise in the sight of my mom and siblings and being a success in life in my own eyes. The list could go on and on. So I was a lot more like Martha than Mary and Jesus had to make me sit down! Through gradually stripping away all the things that I thought were so important, God had to prepare me to receive his provision. With repeated lessons, God had to teach me that he is Jehovah-Jireh, the God who provides. He had to teach me to pant after him alone and not him and something else i.e., a decent house, a good job, a position or title, a college degree. (See Psalm 42:1). I practiced panting after him and something else for so long that I had forgotten how much he really means to me. I have learned to sit down, to trust and to receive from the Lord. I learned to cast all my cares on him, to seek first his kingdom and his righteousness; and that he would give me other stuff besides. God doesn't desire to have you broke, busted and disgusted, but he does desire to have you truly fulfilled by being plugged into Him. God is the one who gives us the ability and the know-how to get wealth. Whether that's through a nine-to-five position, an entrepreneurship, or some other means, he has a plan for you and he wants the best for your life. But he cannot give it to you unless you become still and know (recognize) that he is God. So let's recap some important points to remember:

1) Everybody has needs and desires, but can't receive them unless they learn to sit down
2) Men and women alike have pride issues that must be pushed aside to meet God's condition for blessing
3) God will make his children, his sheep, sit down to receive even if it means stripping what is near and dear away for awhile
4) God isn't trying to hurt you. He cares where you sit and he'll make sure the pasture is green.
5) The purpose of sitting is to receive provision from him Jehovah-Jireh.

Now that we, like the multitude are seated and in the position to receive, let's see what Jesus does with that which is placed in his hand.

Receiving the meager with a heavenly view

Chapter 7

*And he commanded the multitude to sit down on the grass, and took the five loaves, and two fishes, **and looking up to heaven**, he blessed, and brake, and gave the loaves to his disciples, and the disciples to the multitude.*

Matthew 14:19

The masses were seated in groups according to Jesus' instructions. With all eyes trained on the God-man, Jesus, the disciples and the crowd watched with bated breath as he takes those two little fishes and five barley loaves in hand. I don't know what was going through the minds of the onlookers at the time, but I can imagine they were wondering what he was about to do. All afternoon the people had watched as he healed the sick of their many infirmities. Yes, they had intently listened as he shared stirring words that seemed to quicken the soul. Their hearts had been pricked as Jesus challenged them to love their neighbor as they loved themselves.

During his teaching, Jesus might have repeated some of the truths he had taught in his famous sermon on the mount, referenced for us in Matthew chapters five through seven. It was hard to grasp some of the new concepts he had been teaching such as the kingdom of heaven belonged to the poor in spirit. Strong's Dictionary states that those who are poor in spirit "are not lacking in spirit, but have the positive moral quality of humility, realizing they have nothing to offer God but are in need of his free gifts". Jesus had promised blessings, joy and eternal life to those who were humble and had a correct attitude about themselves and God. For those who grieved and mourned, he had promised a blessed state of enviable happiness and comfort from the Father. He also boldly proclaimed blessings to those who were physically, emotionally and spiritually hungry. He promised that these folk would not just be given an appetizer, but be fed to full satisfaction.

Perhaps this very promise was reverberating in their minds as hungry stomachs gnarled and growled while they peered at Jesus holding those few loaves of bread and two tiny little fishes. Wait! He was raising them up. Was he going to offer them to the highest bidder? The crowd was probably mixed with poor and wealthy alike. Certainly some were in a better position to pay for this meal than others. But no, that didn't match Jesus' style. He never seemed to be impressed by wealth or interested in yielding to the whims of the rich. Maybe he was going to toss the food in the air to give every-body an equal chance at scrambling for it. After all, there were no more sick or invalid folk in the crowd since Jesus had already healed everyone present according to Matthew

14:14: "And when Jesus went out He saw a great multitude; and He was moved with compassion for them, and healed their sick."

But if he was going to do that why did he have everyone take the reclining position used in preparation for receiving a meal? No, he definitely had something else in mind as he raised the food and looked up past it toward heaven. It was as if he was looking at something or someone other than the food. There was nothing up there, but the sky. What was he looking at? It makes you wonder if he was recalling the words of the psalmist when he penned Psalm 121:

> *I will lift up mine eyes unto the hills, from whence cometh*
> *my help.*
> *My help cometh from the Lord, which made heaven and*
> *earth. Psalm 121: 1-2*

Yes! He definitely was looking up toward heaven with real expectation in his eyes. It was as if he were looking directly up at God and gratefully offering the little he had just received in his hands back to his heavenly Father. It was amazing to behold the sincerity with which he gave earnest thanks to the Father for the bounty he had just supplied to feed the hungry masses that lay at his feet. Looking at Jesus made the onlookers feel like they were being invited to take a spiritual telescopic view of what Jesus was beholding with ease. It was as if they were being transported into some great meeting in heavenly places. They couldn't see anything, but they could hear and feel his gratitude as he communed with his Father on their behalf. Even the disciples looked on with awe. The disciples were repeatedly awed, as they were made privy to the intimate conversations: the prayers between Jesus and God the Father. If only they could get the hang of this type of two-way conversation. It seemed almost too easy yet at the same time mind-boggling. Is this what Jesus meant that day when they had asked him to teach them how to pray like John's disciples? The readiness in which he responded in the Scriptures makes me believe that to his disciples he hadn't seemed bothered or even inquisitive as to why they

asked. He had simply responded:

> *After this manner therefore pray ye:*
> *Our Father, which art in heaven, Hallowed be thy name.*
> *Thy kingdom come. Thy will be done in earth, as it is in*
> *heaven.*
> *Give us this day our daily bread.*
> *And forgive us our debts as we forgive our debtors.*
> *And lead us not unto temptation, but deliver us from evil:*
> *For thine is the kingdom and the power and the glory*
> *forever. Amen.*
>
> Matthew 6:9-13

Was Jesus now demonstrating an object lesson for them

so they could see how it is done? He must have had a look on

his face that made you think he was holding the undivided

attention and unconditional approval of the Creator of the

Universe. He probably seemed to believe and know with

assurance that there was nothing too small for the Father to

be concerned about or even too hard for him to accomplish.

As Jesus looked toward heaven, his face must have revealed

the look of faith in action. There wasn't a bit of fear,

> *Instead of using our lips to curse the very people and things we long to have blessed, we should follow Jesus' example and learn to breathe life.*

intimidation or worry, as he looked toward heaven. Nor was there a look of cockiness or defiance often seen in the expressions of those who seek the satisfaction of God's hand rather than that of his face. Instead with a calm, humble, but expectant gaze he honored his Father by believing in His Word and His character.

The Scriptures say he blessed them, meaning the loaves and the fishes. The word used for blessed in this case is the same one from which we derive the word eulogy. He spoke well of the two fishes and the five loaves. He didn't look down on them with frustration and disappointment. On the contrary he extolled, praised them and praised God for them. How different from the mental images we construe toward people or things that we feel have fallen short of our expectations. The prophet Zechariah, when referencing the doubtful opinion of others regarding the rebuilding of the temple of Jerusalem, reminded us not to despise the day of small things because with the Lord they become great. (See Zechariah 4:10) Oh! If we could just remember the truth of those words, when dealing with a difficult child, a small income or a troubled marriage. Finally, the word translated as "blessed" in this instance also means he acted kindly and imparted benefits to the fishes and the loaves. So, Jesus spoke well of the food, gave thanks to the Father for the food and pronounced favor/benefits to be given to the food before he lowered it down at the conclusion of his prayer. Instead of using our lips to curse the very people and things we long to have blessed, we should follow Jesus' example and learn to breathe life.

Apparently, Jesus knew the Father had agreed and responded with favor to his petition because when he finished his prayer without hesitance he took a firm grip on the provision and took steps to prepare it for distribution. How many times do we fast, pray, plead and beg God for things, but then walk away expecting little or nothing to happen? Or we begin to rehearse complaints and tales of woe about what happened in the past. One minute we are acting as if we believe the King of Kings is listening and caring about our petitions and in the next we behave as if he is either powerless or indifferent. Such thinking is schizophrenic [the coexistence of contradictory or antagonistic attitudes] or at least double-minded. The book of James says that with such an attitude we should not expect to receive anything from the Lord. "But let him ask in faith, with no doubting, for he who doubts is like a wave of the sea driven and tossed by the wind. For let not that man suppose that he will receive anything form the Lord; he is a double-minded man, unstable in all his ways". (James 1:6-8). During prayer, God gives us a heavenly view of the situation. By faith, he wants us to firmly hold on to what we received from him in heavenly places until they are manifested in the natural world.

Honestly, I struggle with the same dilemma.

Sometimes, I am not in agreement with the Father. His
Word says that if I abide in him and his word abides in me I
can ask what I will and it will be done for me. (John 15:7).

The problem occurs when I don't want

...mustard seed-sized faith has enough power to move mountain-sized problems.

to abide in Him. When I am determined to have things my own way, I
am operating out of the flesh and I am
not abiding in Him. Other times I know
the Father is ready and willing to give
me my petitions, but I slip out of the assurance of walking in
the truth of His Word. I slip out of walking in the Spirit down
into the pit of doubt, whining, grumbling, human reasoning,
rationalization and unbelief. As I shift into that frame of
mind, I am not allowing his Word to abide or rest in me
instead I replaced my faith in God with faith in the bigness
of my circumstance. When I approach prayer with either of

these attitudes, I usually end up frustrated. But when by faith, I refuse to take my eyes off of the Lord and his promises while entrusting my will and heart's desires to him, I come away with an overwhelming peace and victory every time. Faith in the name of Jesus always produces more than expected. After all, Jesus said that mustard seed-sized faith has enough power to move mountain-sized problems.

So Jesus said to them...I say to you, if you have faith as a mustard seed, you will say to this mountain, 'Move from here to there,' and it will move; and nothing will be impossible for you. Matthew 17:20

Jesus invites us along with his apostles to take a close look at Him, the Master. After all the way we have been doing things for so long has not been working, so why keep doing it? Day in and day out we get up, complaining that we have to go to work. We complain about the traffic on the

> *Jesus is inviting us to learn from him by inviting the Lord God into our meager situations.*

way to work. We complain about the distance we have to walk from the parking lot. We complain that the customers get on our nerves and then we complain that the paycheck is too small to cover all our bills. Then we start the process all over again each time adding something else to the complaint pile. It seems like instead of things getting better or staying the same they continue to grow worse. Jesus is inviting us to learn from him by inviting the Lord God into our meager situations.

To begin with, instead of getting out of bed with a grumble, begin the day with a "Thank you Heavenly Father for a brand new day!" Invite the Holy Spirit to guide your thoughts and actions by seeking his direction through reading the Bible and praying. These two steps alone cause us to take a heavenly view and to add a blessing to our day. Next rather than allowing yourself to get into the grumbling mode, find a way to thank God for your job, for the transportation and even for the ability to walk from your car to your place

> *By placing our trust in his guidance and provision, we move out of that impossible place faster and God will make the impossible possible.*

of employment. I know life has some real hardships, which cannot be viewed through rose colored glasses, but keeping our eyes on those things above keeps us in the position to see opportunity when it arrives.

Sometimes when it seems my mind is unusually bent toward negativity, I have to actually keep my mouth shut and put some praise and worship music on so I can remember something to be grateful for. When I am going through a really hard time, making up mind to keep a heavenly view may include praying "Lord, please help me to understand what you are teaching me through this situation". It may include looking up scriptures that deal with the dilemma I am facing and meditating on them day and night. By placing our trust in his guidance and provision, we move out of that impossible place faster and God will make the impossible possible. When Jesus was helping to prepare the disciples for his betrayal and crucifixion, he knew that suffering days were ahead for them. He gave them these words for encouragement: "These things I have spoken unto you, that in me ye might have peace. In the world ye shall have tribulation: but be of good cheer; I have overcome the world." (John 16:33). I think we can also draw strength from this scripture because it reminds us that the Lord knows what we are going through before it happens and he also has overcome whatever is troubling us. As we look toward him he will deliver and cause us to come out on top.

Jesus wants us to learn and pattern our actions after what he does. By holding up the loaves to bless them, he enabled everyone around to see what he was doing. He is not trying to keep us in the dark on how to receive what we need. On the contrary, he invites us to follow his pattern. He wants us to understand and appreciate what it means to bless that which we hold in our hands. Appreciation and thankfulness for the meager things in life make room for more. Jesus also wants us to understand that we must fix our gaze on heaven with our hearts. Then we will behold the great size and power of the Provider, rather than locking our gaze on the problem right before our eyes and being deceived by the appearance of its size.

God who is unseen to the naked eye is greater than any and everything we can see with our eyes. But we can only see the hand of God by faith in him, which comes by hearing or receiving truth in our hearts. That hearing or receiving can only come by learning the truth found in God's Word as is stated in Romans 10:17: "So then faith comes by hearing, and hearing by the word of God." By reading and meditating on God's word we learn the truth about his all knowing, all loving, all powerful, omni-present and everlasting character. We learn his principles for working in the lives of men on the earth. We also learn to trust that he is always willing and ready to work in our own individual lives. If we don't learn to hear the Word and receive that faith in Christ, we will grope around miserably living beneath our privilege and not accessing the things God has provided for his children.

For a very long time I limited the things God could do for me because I kept allowing this world's way of thinking to dominate my mind. I refused to believe God could use me to make a difference in the world. I figured the only way I could survive was to return back to the very work God had called me from because I didn't think I was capable of doing anything else. In a sense I was trying desperately to do the same thing Peter and the other disciples did shortly after Jesus had arisen from the grave. Confused and discouraged, they returned to fishing even though Jesus had said follow me and I will make you fishers of men. I was such a creature of habit that I thought I could not change or discipline myself to do what I needed to do to succeed in ministry. The Holy Spirit had to keep reminding me to become changed by getting a new mindset. I had to throw out the lies. Satan is a liar! You and I can do all things through Christ who strengthens us (Philippians 4:13). I have decided to follow my Savior's lead by taking a heavenly view of my life and holding on to the visions and promises God has shown me securely until they are manifested in my life.

Blessed, Broken and Given Back for Service

Chapter 8

*And when he had taken the five loaves and the two fishes, he looked up to heaven, **and blessed, and brake the loaves, and gave them** to his disciples to set before them; and the two fishes divided he among them all.*   *Mark 6:41*

Who doesn't enjoy the words, bounty and blessings? Bounty implies generosity or having more than enough and blessings refer to favor, good fortune, approval or any thing that brings happiness. Sounds like something everyone would want to have a part of. Indeed we like to think about the bountiful blessings, the spiritual maturity and the changed character, but few want to participate in the process necessary to become a blessing. It's sort of like the old adage that says, "Everyone wants to go to heaven, but nobody wants to die".

Let's see what we can learn about the process of purification and preparation for service from Jesus' handling of the loaves and the fishes. Although we talked about the definition of the word "blessed" in the previous chapter, I want to take a closer look at the word in order to grasp a better understanding of its use in the Synoptic renderings of this event. Matthew, Mark and Luke stress that right after Jesus took the loaves in his hand, he looked up to heaven and blessed them. Previously, I mentioned that the Greek word we translate as blessed is *'eulogeo'* which generally means to speak kindly of, to be grateful for or to praise. There is more to this word, however, than the brief definitions involving praise and gratefulness. It also means to consecrate and to impart benefits to the one being blessed. So when Mark 6:41 says the Lord looked up to heaven and blessed them, Mark is indicating that Jesus consecrated the loaves or set them apart as holy for a sacred or serious use. He also added or imparted some benefits from his divine nature into them.

Somewhere in between the time the loaves left the hands of the little boy and entered to the disciples' hands for distribution, the loaves and the fishes were changed. Previously, the loaves had been baked with the intention of being a little snack lunch, but now the Lord had commissioned them to do a much larger job. Similarly, when the Lord asks us to present our bodies as "a living sacrifice, holy and acceptable unto God, which is [our] reasonable service" (Romans 12:1), He is asking that we willingly surrender our lives to be consecrated

> *...until we surrender to his Lordship we cannot experience the full satisfaction of a yielded life.*

for his use. When we are born again, we become new creations. Until we surrender to his Lordship, however, we cannot experience the full satisfaction of a yielded life. Nor are we able to accomplish the great things he has designed for us if we do not live our lives under the control of the Spirit.

When we receive Christ, the Holy Spirit comes to live in us and certain spiritual gifts are imparted to us by the Lord:

> *But unto each one of us is given grace according to the measure of the gift of Christ. Wherefore he saith, When he ascended up on high, he led captivity captive, and gave gifts unto men. ...For the perfecting of the saints, for the work of the ministry, for the edifying of the body of Christ. Ephesians 4:7-8 & 13*

Therefore, to utilize these gifts for the body of Christ we must learn to walk in the Spirit. Just as the loaves were consecrated to be properly used by God, so will we be consecrated, as we entrust our lives to his holy hands. As long as we try to control our own lives, we allow ourselves to be misused by Satan.

My grandmother once told me a story about a precious gift of hers that was misused. One of my uncles, who had gone to Germany during his tour of duty in the army, brought her a fine linen tablecloth home as a gift. His younger brother, not recognizing the value of the gift, thought it was just a piece of fabric and used it to polish his motorcycle. As a result he ruined a section of the tablecloth. When she told me, I was shocked to hear that he was so insensitive and had done such a thing. But in a sense we misuse something far more valuable than a tablecloth every day. When we do and say dishonest or ungodly things, we misuse our bodies and limit our own usefulness.

I didn't realize how serious God is about righteousness until I began to ask God to use me and to make me more like him. I had no idea that he would begin to re-condition my heart to become more sensitive to the promptings of the Holy Spirit. For example, the things I used to do without a qualm, I can no longer get away with. I used to reason that it was okay to take the post-its or pens from the office because I figured they were my supplies and they belonged to me anyway. Now I get convicted of stealing. Little things I used

> *...the more we stay connected, through prayer, reading, obeying and quick repentance, the better, more useful and joyful we become.*

to call "bending the rules" are not acceptable and the Holy Spirit convicts me to live according to a higher standard. Things I used to be able to say during a debate or argument will now eat at me until I repent and apologize. Of course, the sanctification process is on-going in a Christian's life, so there will always be room for growth and change. The wonderful truth is that the more we stay connected through prayer, reading, obeying and quick repentance, the better, more useful and joyful we become.

Like the loaves of bread became consecrated, holy and satisfactory simply by being held and blessed by Jesus, so will our lives become consecrated, holy and acceptable as we allow him to hold and bless us. The book of John doesn't use this word 'blessed', but uses the words 'gave thanks' instead. The word 'thanks" implies profuse or freely given gratitude for the loaves and the fishes. As we interpret these words from scripture, we can draw some exciting conclusions. Like the bread, Jesus blesses us. He appreciates and rejoices over us, acts kindly toward and speaks well of us. He imparts benefits to us and he desires to consecrate us for his own divine use as well. Considering all this, the blessing part doesn't seem so bad, does it? As some of the kids I know would say, "I can get down with that!" It's the next part of the preparation process, "the breaking", that is a bit more distasteful.

No one likes the thought of being broken in anyone's grip—not even in the firm, but loving grip of Jesus. However, as we continue to look at the five loaves of bread and the two fishes we see that the prerequisite to profound use and multiplication was the breaking. As I researched the word break as used in three of the Gospel accounts, I found Matthew used a very different word than Mark and Luke. Matthew used the word that meant "to break in pieces or to break off pieces" while Mark and Luke used a word that indicates breaking in a certain manner, i.e. a breaking down. Jesus had

such a distinct way of breaking bread that his disciples rec-

ognized him after his resurrection simply by watching the

way he broke the bread. (See Luke

24:30-31)

Jesus also has a special way of

breaking us to make us suitable for

> ...*the prerequisite to profound use and multiplication was the breaking.*

service. Some of the definitions of break found in Webster's

dictionary really came together to form a vivid picture of the

breaking process: 1) to smash, split, crack; 2) to cut open the

surface of soil, skin, 3) to tame as with force, 4) to get rid of

(habit); 5) to make bankrupt; 6) to interrupt (a journey); 7)

to penetrate silence, darkness, and 8) to decipher or solve.

The definitions make the process of breaking sound painful,

and it is, but it is also promising because the latter definitions

indicate refining, perfecting and discovering of purpose.

I had my own plans for being a useful servant to the

Lord. I think my plan included me being served more than

being used to serve. I wanted to serve the Lord on my terms without experiencing any discomfort. When my marriage ended it seemed like a sledge hammer came crushing down on me. Talk about feeling smashed and cut open. Now, hear me, the Lord doesn't desire divorce for any us. He'd rather us repent and forgive one another. The Scriptures make it clear that God hates divorce, but he doesn't let any of life's painful situations go to waste either. The divorce was the consequence of sin, but the Omniscient Lord knew all about its coming and he allowed it to bring me to a place of emotional bankruptcy so I could learn to totally trust him to order my steps. He also used the whole experience to refine me and to give me direction and purpose.

> ...the process of breaking sound painful, and it is, but...promising ... refining, perfecting and discovering of purpose.

I was content living a life defined by my husband's world. I was a Christian and I loved the Lord. I was a pastor's wife who went to church every Sunday and several times during the week. We were actively sharing the message of Christ in the community and on the job, but I still was living a defeated life. Deep inside, I measured my value or self-worth based on being his wife, keeping him happy and being a success in the opinion of others. While trying to stay Mrs. H. and keeping up appearances, I took far too much abuse for far too long. I made excuses for his womanizing and tolerated his behaviors that were being driven by pornography's lust demon. I am ashamed to say, I let Satan misuse me by believing the lie that it was my fault he behaved as he did. I felt I had failed him as a wife. I internalized the guilt and shame even when I received a call from one of his lovers naming all the women he had had affairs with in the past—people that only he and I had known. Instead of being angry with him, I hated myself and the women who had yielded to his advances. When she said they talked and laughed about my fat body and that he only stayed with me because of the kids, I felt humiliated, but readily received his lying words that she was lying and upset because he had just broken off the affair with her.

My husband was quite manipulative and I was quite foolish. He knew just the right words to say, to make me feel guilty for losing my temper with him for his unfaithfulness. Most often, I would end up feeling like I wasn't sexy enough, good-looking enough or a good enough wife and mother. For the longest time I convinced myself, against the truth, that Jesus wanted me to fight for my marriage by continuing to endure until my husband changed. I was convinced that he really wanted to do right, but couldn't help himself. My compromises almost destroyed me, mentally, emotionally, physically and spiritually, but my journey was about to be abruptly interrupted by force.

After I answered my call to ministry God began to wake me early in the mornings for prayer. It seemed the more I sought to know God's will for me, the stronger I became. My husband became very agitated because I would slip out of bed before day break to pray in the living room. When I'd leave the room he would be sound asleep, but when I returned he'd be angry and swear that I had disturbed his rest by leaving the bed. As I continued to live a life more controlled by God's Spirit, I gained strength to say no to my husband's whims. When he began to stay out all night again as he had during previous flings, I wanted to continue to honor my marriage vows, but became fearful of getting sick again. I told him I would no longer be intimate with him without protection, because I didn't trust him. It was a matter of control for him, so he refused to be intimate under those conditions. Despite that I continued to believe our marriage was going to survive.

As my self-esteem began to grow, I still loved, prayed for and supported my husband, but I would not cover up for him anymore. I refused to run away from the church God had called me to serve in because he had gotten caught in another affair and had chosen to resign. God gave me the courage to confront my husband about his unfaithfulness quietly, but firmly. I told him God wanted us to be holy and if he wanted to stay with me he would have to stop staying out and sleeping around. He said he didn't think we were traveling on the same path anymore and he was leaving. He stopped hiding his affair and filed for a divorce. When it happened, I wandered around for a long time feeling displaced and feeling like I was totally exposed and vulnerable.

Thank God! I have come to realize that Jesus had me in the palm of his hand all the time. During the process, the Lord broke off some stupid ideas I had about myself that were limiting me from enjoying life and freely sharing the love and vic-

> *The divorce forced me to begin to walk in the truth I had been quoting all along.*

tory in Christ with others. He helped me to stop living a disconnected double life. To others I quoted scripture and indicated that I believed I could do all things through Christ who strengthens me, but when it came to my husband I was a wimp and I thought I was a victim of the circumstances. The divorce forced me to begin to walk in the truth I had been quoting all along. I pray that someone can learn from my life that God has much better for you than settling for a life far less than what he designed.

No woman or man deserves to be misused and abused physically, verbally or emotionally. In a heterosexual marriage, the only marital union the Lord sanctifies and approves of, God intended for the man and the woman to respect and cherish each other. I digress to discuss heterosexual marriage because Satan has deceived so many to believe that they were born homosexual or convinced them that these types of relationships are pleasing to God. Surely God loves all of us whether we are walking in obedience to his will or not, but God is holy. He has a righteous standard and homosexual behavior is against his will for mankind. He has the power to deliver us from this type of bondage just as he has power to deliver from every other form of sinful bondage. Satan is quite deceptive and one of his best tricks is to convince us that we are doing right by distorting the truth of God's word. But God is gracious and he will help us to overcome any and every sin or stumbling block, if we allow him. God has sanctified marriage as representative of the relationship between Christ and the Church. I still believe in God's plan and celebrate the sanctity of marriage. It is a wonderful state for a man and woman to walk out the plan of God for their lives. Both husband and wife are to submit to each other in the fear of the Lord, even though God has established a definite order for the home. The husband is to love, cherish and give himself for the wife as Christ does the Church. The wife is to honor and submit to her husband as the head, but that submission should never supersede obedience to the Lord.

In every marriage there will be disagreements and areas for growth, but neither partner should be misused or abused. Many people are suffering things behind closed doors in the name of Christianity, but the Lord is not in it. Satan, the thief, came to steal, kill and to destroy. Jesus, our Savior, came that we might have life and that we might have it more abundantly. I used to think there was something so wrong with me; therefore I thought I couldn't enjoy a life of significance and real peace in Christ. It was a long time before the Lord could break down the strongholds Satan had on my mind. At one time in my life, every other sentence out of my mouth was I'm sorry!, I think at one time I was sorry that I was alive. I felt like I couldn't complete anything and I would always manage to derail my own success. That was a lie from the Pit, that I had embraced for much too long. But Hallelujah! Jesus has penetrated my cell of darkness. He has set me free and I am walking in the liberty Christ has given to me. With that new found freedom, I now find that it's okay not to be perfect. I realize that I have areas that I need to grow in, but I am content to know that Jesus is working them out in me. It also helps me to be more patient with others. So my breaking turned into a break-

through that took me to the next

step of being given back.

Many people are suffering things behind closed doors in the name of Christianity, but the Lord is not in it.

When Jesus had finished

breaking the blessed bread, he

handed it back to the disciples to distribute to those who

were seated in groups of fifty. The bread had been placed in

Jesus' hand as ordinary, but it returned to the disciples' hands

transformed. Now, somehow it was multiplying! I don't

know how it was done. Perhaps a piece was being broken off

and another piece replaced it. All I know is that what began

as scarcely enough for a little boy's lunch was changed to a

bountiful supply for the masses.

Instead you will be able to give out of the sufficiency of Christ.

When the Lord breaks through

our walls that keep us imprisoned

he equips us to be given away

in service to others as well. The breaking often exposes a

part of our life that we would usually keep hidden, but God

uses that embarrassing factor of our life as a tool to help others overcome defeat. Sometimes, like bread, you may be given away by freely sharing your love and testimony with a neighbor or with someone in distress. You may actually become more effective at whatever you do: teaching, preaching, managing, parenting, or whatever. The Lord will use us in all different types of ways. The difference is you will no longer operate out of self-sufficiency with a fear of failure and depletion. Instead you will be able to give out of the sufficiency of Christ. I think the best benefit is the fact that after being broken, you are free to really enjoy life in the service of the Lord. Even though we are limited and in many ways frail, there is no lack in Christ. As we learn to become comfortable resting in his ability, God will use us under his anointing, his strength and his all-sufficiency. So there is no need to be afraid to freely share what he has given to us with others.

Give It As He Gives It to You

Chapter 9

*And Jesus took the loaves; and when he had given thanks,
he distributed to the disciples, and the disciples to them
that were set down; and likewise of the fishes as much as
they would.*   *John 6:11*

Throughout the Gospels, which contain accounts of
the feeding of the five thousand, the title "apostle"
and "disciple" are used interchangeably for Jesus' hand-
picked twelve. I thought it was noteworthy, however, that all
four gospel writers referred to the twelve only as "disciples"
in this setting. Each title signifies a different aspect of their
position. For instance, the word "disciple" literally means a
learner, one who follows one's teacher. Each disciple was a

pupil, who learned from closely watching and adhering to the Master's words and his actions. Therefore, a disciple was expected to imitate his teacher.

On the other hand, the word "apostle", literally means one sent forth. Even though they had been recognized as apostles, I believe they realized that they would always remain Jesus' disciples. When Jesus sent the twelve forth to preach the gospel, to cast out spirits, and to heal all manner of diseases he called them apostles. They were given authority and instructions on what to say, where to go, what to do, and how to do it. They were told to share the Word, healing and deliverance freely because they had received freely from him. They had heard Jesus preach, seen him heal and seen him cast out devils, but never had they been asked or commissioned to take part in so great a miracle as this.

When Jesus had originally told them that he expected them to feed this massive crowd, he knew the magnitude of the task was beyond their imagination or their level of faith.

The Scriptures said that he knew all along what he would do, but his disciples didn't. "But he said this to test him, for He Himself knew what He would do," (John 6:6). This was definitely uncharted territory for them and they timidly followed his directions. Can't you envision this awesome sight? Pharisees and sinners, rich and poor, adults and children, all seated side by side on the grass. The only distinction between those being served was the size of the group. No more than 50 or 100 were allowed in a group. No one was given a special seat or place. The only requirement for being fed was to be humbly seated on the ground. As the disciples were closest to Jesus, they would have been the first to see the miracle in progress. They were awed and glad to imitate him as he began to dole out food for each of them to distribute. It probably felt great just to be able to participate. The disciples quickly moved from the place of being overwhelmed by a huge problem to becoming part of the solution. They no longer were gripped with fear. All they had to do was follow Jesus' words. Jesus may have said, Peter you take this basket of bread and pass it out to the group on the left. John you carry the fish. Andrew, you take this basket to that group and so on and so forth. Can't you imagine the disciples beaming as they proudly walked to each group and said, "Help yourself there is enough for everybody. There's plenty more where this comes from".

Everyone likes to be on the winning team. They didn't understand any more than the people they were serving how Jesus did it, but they were just glad to be identified as one of his disciples. They ran and served each and every person in the groups just as they were instructed. Jesus had already done the real work and they had the honor of being a part of it. All they had to do was give it away. They probably had to make several trips with seconds and thirds because all four of the Gospel accounts say they didn't stop distributing food till the crowd was well fed.

That day, the twelve had learned well the key elements of being a good disciple: 1) faithfully follow Jesus' words, 2) follow his ways – imitate him; 3) give to others freely the way you received it; 4) be willing and be quick to serve; and 5) keeping the faith, do not get weary in well doing. As simplistic as it sounds, that basically is what we have to do.

I believe the word imitate is just as significant for us today as it was for Jesus' disciples then. Like the Twelve, we can also become fearful and overwhelmed by the pressures of life, personal

> *1) faithfully follow Jesus' words,*
> *2) follow his ways – imitate him;*
> *3) give to others freely the way you received it;*
> *4) be willing and be quick to serve;*
> *5) keeping the faith, do not get weary in well doing.*
> *… that is what we have to do.*

tragedies and the masses of hurting people in the World. God doesn't want us to continue walking about in fear, but to walk in love and faith instead as indicated in I John 4:17-18:

Herein is our love made perfect, that we may have bold-ness in the day of judgment: because as he is, so are we in this world. There is no fear in love; but perfect love casteth out fear: because fear hath torment. He that feareth is not made perfect in love.

I was always so fearful even when I put on the front of being courageous. I often felt convicted by this scripture, not understanding that it was simply saying that we can rest in the assurance of God's love. He is committed to us. He will never leave us nor forsake us and he will always be our deliverance. His love is as sure as his character. Therefore, if we received him as our Lord and Savior, we can walk in the confidence of his love. We will and should remain fearful, if we are relying upon our own ability to save, sustain and to deliver us. We should also be fearful if we have placed our trust in man, money or power. But remember, the five thousand were fed by the power of God's love. Satan was defeated at Calvary by the power of God's love and the Lord promised that we are in him and nothing will ever be able to

separate us from the power of that love.

> *Nay, in all these things we are more than conquerors through him that loved us. For I am persuaded, that neither death, nor life, nor angels, nor principalities, nor powers, nor things present, nor things to come, nor height, nor depth, nor any other creature, shall be able to separate us from the love of God, which is in Christ Jesus our Lord.*
>
> Romans 8:37-39

God's word contains everything we need for life eternal

and life victorious. The principles contained in God's Holy

Word work. If we consistently apply them in our daily lives, we will have what the Bible says we can have. Jesus said ask.

> *We need to remain fearful, if we are relying upon our own ability to save, sustain and to deliver us. We should also be fearful if we have placed our trust in man, money or power.*

He said that if we abide in Him and his words abide in us, we

can ask what we will and it will be done for us. He can't lie

because he is God. So, what do we have to lose? I believe

Jesus walked on earth for thirty-three and a half years to set a pattern for us to follow. He could have died for our sins without having to stay here on earth for such a long time, but I believe he chose to show us how to live life as a child and as an adult.

As his disciples, we are directed to imitate him as we live life by the power of the Holy Spirit. Just trying to do the things Jesus did in our own strength doesn't work. If we could live a holy life by simply having the will to do it, we wouldn't have needed Jesus to redeem us. As we walk through this life as a born again believer, only then are we able to trust in God and his promises. As a disciple we are equipped to follow Jesus' ways: to live a life of prayer, to obey the will of God (learned through studying the Scriptures and being led by the Holy Spirit), to freely share the Good News, to pray for the healing and deliverance of others regardless of their station in life, and to overcome the temptation to become weary while doing the will of God. Sounds easy, right?

You and I both know that living the Christian life isn't as easy as all that. We are in a real battle, called spiritual warfare, that works overtime at undermining our faith, keeping trouble in our families and strife in our churches: "For we wrestle not against flesh and blood, but against principalities, against powers, against the rulers of the darkness of this world, against spiritual wickedness in high places" (Ephesians 6:12). Satan tries to make life difficult by criticizing and attempting to muzzle Christians in the media, in the workplace and in his own mind. He tries to convince us that the message of Christ is antiquated and irrelevant. Or he attacks our minds or character in an attempt to convince us that we are unworthy to share Christ's message with others. The only thing that will liberate men and women in this world is the message of God's grace and their decision to receive eternal life through the Living Bread his Son: "For God so loved the world that he gave his only begotten Son that whosoever believeth in him shall not perish but shall have everlasting life," (John 3:16). Jesus finished the hard

work already! Our job is to imitate the Master and freely

give the Bread away to any and all who will receive it.

Everybody Eats! Everybody's Satisfied!

Chapter 10

And they did all eat, and were filled.   Mark 6:42

Do you know how difficult it is to prepare a large meal that is palatable to everyone's tastes? Normally there are, at most six people seated around a family dinner table and it is difficult to get them all to agree on the meat and the potatoes. Inevitably, someone plays around with their vegetables, passes on dessert, frowns at the chicken or makes the declaration, "I'm not hungry!" Today, it is a major undertaking to manage to get everyone to the table at the same time. Not only did Jesus have everyone seated and still for a meal, but he has over five thousand folks licking their lips and patting their full bellies. That's what I call serving a meal!

As we have delved into the various accounts of this momentous event, I think we should consider the relevance of the meal having being appropriate or suitable for everyone at the scene. We know that there was only one course to the meal: small fish and barley bread loaf pieces. We know the food was cold because it had been carried around all day and the Scriptures stated the day was far spent. We also know that there were five thousand men besides the women and the children. So, what made this meal so thoroughly satisfying to so many people? I think the answer lies in the fact that they had received food specifically prepared and blessed by the Creator of the Universe. No one knows us better than the one who made us. He knows what

> *No one knows us better than the one who made us. He knows what we need as well as what we want.*

we need as well as what we want. Most of the time we go without just because we refuse to ask and receive what he has to offer. The same One, who gave us the breath of life and caused us to become a living soul, is the only one who really understands us and knows how to fulfill our deepest longings. Yes, he knew then and he knows now what everyone needs.

The crowd probably consisted of everyone from dignitaries who had grown accustomed to delectable cuisine to the common fisherman to even a beggar or two who would have been content with a crust of stale bread for the night. Just as he did on that evening in Palatine, Jesus offers life-giving sustenance to any and everyone who is willing to partake. These people had to take their minds off who they were sitting next to, who was serving them and even the manner in which they were being served. Their focus had to shift to primarily getting some of that life giving bread and fish. To receive, they had to be willing to open their hearts, their hands and their mouths. Although it was unbelievable and made no logical sense because they had been so famished prior to eating, now they were completely full and satisfied. Looking at the meager fare that had

Just as he did on that evening in Palatine, Jesus offers life- giving sustenance to any and everyone who is willing to partake.

been offered to Jesus, you would have assumed that there would not be enough to whet the appetite of a few, let alone satisfy the stomachs of them all. But that's how Jesus works. He is El Shaddai, the All Sufficient One, after all.

When a person trusts Jesus to supply what they need, they end up feeling completely full like we used to after Sunday dinner with Grandma. On those Sunday afternoons, you couldn't put another bite in your mouth, even if you tried. That's what it means to be really full. One of the Gospel writers said the food was set before the multitude and they could eat as much as they wanted. I believe that is what the Lord is offering to every man, woman and child on the planet. He is offering abundant life and it is there for the taking. Jesus later told the same crowd, the next day after this miracle, that they were seeking for bread that would perish. He said that there was bread that could sustain any hunger: the true Bread of Life which the Father had sent:

> *For the bread of God is he which cometh down from heaven, and giveth life unto the world. And Jesus said unto them, I am the bread of life: he that cometh to me shall never hunger; and he that believeth on me shall never thirst. John 6:33, 35.*

The people in the crowd had worked up a hearty appetite. They could see, taste, touch and smell the miraculously transformed bread and fish they so gladly ate. Unfortunately, the next day many did not partake of the Everlasting Bread he was offering because it required faith and surrender of their hearts to the One who had made them. We forget that the things we see are made up of things we cannot see and we often get stumped by depending upon our five senses. The scriptures that are often used to define faith bear this out:

*Now faith is the substance of things hoped for, the evi-
dence of things not seen. Through faith we understand
that the worlds were framed by the word of God, so that
things which are seen were not made of things which do
appear. Hebrews 11:1 & 3*

I think we need to fully comprehend that even as believers
our faith is not just for the sweet by and by, but it is also for
an abundantly full and satisfying life here and now. The Lord
wants us to continually partake of his Holy Word so we can
receive the truths and principles that will affect our deci-
sions and the conditions in which we live. By continually
communing with and daily partaking of the bread of life,
we will remain satisfied to the full and have enough to share
with others. Just as the worlds were framed by the word of
God, our minds, hearts and lives will also be redirected and
framed to conform to the image of his Son.

As a non-believer, we have a choice to eat or to pass
up the Living Bread, Jesus, and to be filled or to go hungry
not possessing eternal life. As a believer, we also have a

choice to daily eat God's Word, in order to stay full, grow

and abound or we can choose to partake just barely enough

to get by. If we make the latter choice, I am convinced that

we will not know the contentment of being filled to the full

with all the Lord has to offer us and we will not successfully

leave a bread crumb trail for the world to taste and see that

the Lord is good.

Gather Up the Fragments –
Don't Lose Them

Chapter 11

When they were filled, he said unto his disciples, <u>Gather</u> up the <u>fragments</u> that <u>remain</u>, that nothing be <u>lost</u>. Therefore, they gathered them together, and <u>filled</u> <u>twelve</u> baskets with the fragments of the five barley loaves, which remained over and above unto them that had eaten.

John 6:12-13

W hen I first read this passage in John chapter six, I was bewildered by the directions Jesus gave his disciples just minutes after he had finished feeding everyone in that massive crowd. He pointedly told them to collect each and every broken fragment from the grassy eating area. I wondered why Jesus was so concerned about a few crumbs when he could have made more fish and bread anytime he wanted to? Was he being overly cautious about wastefulness? Was he simply making sure the picnic area was left neat and tidy? Or did he have a greater intent?

At first, this command made very little sense to me, in view of the great event that had taken place. Considering the fact that it was the end of a very long day and his disciples were probably exhausted from making the several trips necessary to serve all those people, this seemed like an unnecessary expense of energy. But the Holy Spirit reminded me that these fragments were not just ordinary morsels of bread and fish anymore. These were anointed fragments. Every single one of them had passed through the Lord's hand and they had value. They represented the blessings of God in the same way that the Lord had spoken at the beginning of the earth and said "Let there be..." and there was.

Jesus had lifted the loaves and fish, speaking good over them and they became multiplied blessings. I am sure everyone who had felt famished hours earlier would testify that those fragments of bread and fish had become a blessing to them. Now, according to the Scriptures, their bellies were full and there was no room left for another bite. Apparently, no one thought to pocket some of the morsels for later, but feeling satisfied—they just left them lying on the grass. However, the intrinsic value of the discarded fragments was not lessened simply because the people's desire and appreciation for them was diminished. Remember, earlier I said that when the Lord held the loaves up in the air, he had divinely blessed them. Therefore to leave the morsels strewn on the grass would have been a serious waste and a misuse of their intended purpose.

Although we don't know the exact words Jesus spoke in his prayer, in essence he asked God to use that which was about to be consumed so that those who consume it may praise God. (Zodiahaities, The Complete Word Study Dictionary, p.677). Think about the many blessings God has given us in our lives that we receive for the moment, but quickly let fall to the ground when the initial excitement wears off. Myriads of promises have come to pass in our lives that we could continually share to strengthen the hearts of others, but we have simply left them strewn on the ground in pursuit of something else. Certainly, I have been guilty of the same carelessness exhibited by this mixed multitude.

For instance, I stumbled across an entry in one of my old journals written about three years ago. I had received this prophecy from the Lord while I was living with my sister's family. Although they were wonderful to me, I was feeling desperately like a failure because I wanted my own home again or even an apartment and I didn't see any way I could manage it. This is what I was given during prayer:

> *When we neglect to rehearse the blessings of the Lord, we can begin to take them for granted in the same manner that those who had eaten of the fish and the loaves took those fragments for granted.*

Write the words that I tell you in a book. You are my prophet, says the Lord. I will provide for you for you have trusted in my Word and you have not lifted up your soul unto vanity. Although you have been tempted and tried, you have come forth in your faith as pure gold. Praise ye me all your days and make melody in your heart for your captivity has been turned. As to your living quarters, I shall provide you with a place of beauty and bounty. Men shall cry in awe as to how you acquired it and ye shall sing my praises saying "This is the goodness of the Lord to them that put their trust in Him!" Fear not, neither let yourself doubt for your deliverance draweth nigh. Listen to further instructions. Do not trust the words of men. I shall reveal my Word directly to my prophet. You need not fear. I will not desert you and neither will I forsake you. Have not I been faithful in the past to give you the desires of your heart? [I answered] Yes, my Lord you have. My daughter, I know this time of testing has been difficult, but you have now entered into my rest. I have seen to it. You thought you had to do it, but it was the work of My Hand. You are My handiwork and My responsibility. Trust ye in Me, thus saith the Lord. Now be still and see the salvation of the Lord, Yahweh. Dear Lord, I bless your Most Holy Name. There is no one like you in all the Earth; nor in the heavens above. Your ways are perfect and they are just. How good you are, oh Lord! Your infinite mercies and tender-kindness lasts unto all generations. It is a good thing to trust in You and to sing praises to Your Name. You are my Hope. You are my sure salvation. You redeemed me and my offspring by the blood of your own dear Son, my Lord and my Savior Jesus Christ— God the Son, Holy and Majestic. King of Kings and Lord of Lords is He. You have filled me with your precious Holy Spirit. You have caused rivers of living water to flow from my belly- a ceaseless fountain. Though I could never be worthy of you myself because my righteousness is as filthy rags, You saw fit to make me acceptable by the supreme sacrifice—the cleansing blood of Your Son. Your Son, who continually maketh intercession for me daily. You teach me, train me and discipline me by your Spirit who indwells me and tells me to go to the right or to the left. I will not fret, but trust and depend upon You. The Lord says, "Do not try to make a name for yourself. I will cause your name to be blessed. You glorify Me. I will prosper you and exalt you, saith the Lord."

[Remember] The Lord wants his children to be called, "trees of righteousness, the planting of the Lord that he might be glorified," Isaiah 61:3. Trees are land-markers that the wayfarer might find his or her way. Trees bring shade and shelter in the storm. They draw heavily upon life-giving water and provide water-filled fruit to sustain those who partake. Trees stand tall and act as an anchor to those who hold on to them.

That entry was written in the fall of 2004 and I walked into my brand new town home in April of 2005. For a while, I rehearsed the miraculous way God had provided it to me, but then over time I became pre-occupied with the pressing cares of the present. The Lord had blessed me to acquire my home through personal hard work, help and encouragement of family and friends all of which came through his gracious hands. Although I walked through my doors daily, to my shame, I found myself reflecting less and less on the fulfillment of the great personal promise God had made to me. When we neglect to rehearse the blessings of the Lord, we can begin to take them for granted in the same manner that those who had eaten of the fish and the loaves took those fragments for granted. In the Old Testament, God had the children of Israel to rehearse his miraculous interventions aloud for the benefit of their present and future generations.

And thou shalt remember all the way which the Lord thy God led thee these forty years in the wilderness, to humble thee and to prove thee, to know what was in thine heart, whether thou wouldest keep his commandments, or no. And he hungered thee, and suffered thee to hunger, and fed thee with manna, which thou knewest not, neither did thy fathers know; that he might make thee know that man doth not live by bread only, but by every word that proceedeth out of the mouth of the Lord doth man live. Thy raiment waxed not old upon thee, neither did thy foot swell, these forty years. Deuteronomy 8: 2-4

I believe he calls us to do the same so that all who hear and see, in other words partake of the blessing, will praise God's Name. God gave me so many provisions of food, shelter, health, transportation, work and love so that I would not forget it but rehearse his goodness in the ears of others. As a result, they will realize the infinite love God has toward us. That's only one of the lessons I learned from the fragments.

Secondly, God pointed out that regardless of its size and condition, He, the Lord Jesus, cares about every morsel of his creation. This truth can be applied to the bread and loaves, but most importantly it pertains to people. Like these morsels, broken people may have been discarded, pushed aside and forgotten about by others, but never by God. Even people who are difficult to live with like the moody, the mean, and the phony are not discarded by the Lord because he loves and wants an eternal intimate relationship with each of us. This is how Jesus expressed it in John 6:39-40:

> *This is the will of the Father who sent Me, that of all He has given Me I should lose nothing, but should raise it up at the last day. "And this is the will of Him who sent Me, that everyone who sees the Son and believes in Him may have everlasting life; and I will raise him up at the last day."*

I believe God wants each of us modern-day disciples to take personally Jesus' commandment given to the twelve, "...Gather up the fragments that none be lost". The word "gather" means to assemble together, to invite, call together, pick up. Sometimes I have heeded the promptings of the Holy Spirit and reached out to gather the lost, but other times I have failed miserably in this area. Thankfully, God never fails. He never meets a person he doesn't know how to help and he never gets tired or deserts those who call on his Name. People who have lost their hope of a better life or who have made some wrong choices about friends, lovers, finances and substance abuse are all valuable in the eyes of the Lord. Some folks may be larger than life in society while others may lay homeless and nameless in a dark alley, but they all matter greatly to Christ. The Lord cares about all of us, the fat, the skinny, the short and the tall. Everybody has been created in God's own image with a divine purpose in mind. He cares enough to gather us to himself, pick us up, clean us up and regenerate us with everlasting life, if only we will let Him.

Maybe, you have never been physically beaten, abused, destitute, addicted or deserted. Maybe you have been so blessed that you have never had a 'down and out' experience in life, but if you have never entered into a personal relationship with Jesus Christ, you are still fragmented. In fact, until we make Jesus our Savior we can be nothing but fragmented, broken and lost no matter how much we try to fool others and ourselves. Only through faith in Christ can we be made whole. Jesus often makes reference to the term "whole" when discussing the healing and restoration of a sick person who was diseased, crippled etc. "When Jesus heard it, he saith unto them, They that are whole have no need of the physician, but they that are sick: I came not to call the righteous, but sinners to repentance", (Mark 2:17).

In this verse, we see that Jesus correlates sickness with unrighteousness and wholeness with righteousness (being in right standing with God). He isn't talking about physical illness here, but spiritual sickness. We have all been fragmented, broken, diseased and crippled by sin and are unable to make ourselves complete, healthy or whole without intervention from the Great Physician, Jesus Christ! Our thoughts, bodies and our world have been warped by sin. We find it hard to trust and to believe in the very one who came to deliver us. Consequently, we stay in bondage and carry burdens that God wants to deliver us from. When a person is unsaved, he remains broken and dead in sin awaiting judgment because of an unwillingness to receive the free gift of eternal life offered by Christ. However, when and if that person opens his heart to receive by faith the message of Christ, he is immediately blessed with a new nature, a new future and a new destination. "Therefore, if anyone is in Christ, he is a new creation; old things have passed away; behold all things have become new (2 Corinthians 5:17 NKJV).

The believer receives immediate and lasting benefits in trade for the old sinful life:

1. Instead of being an enemy of God, he becomes a child of God;

2. Instead of stumbling about making a mess of his life and going from bad to worse, God will work out his divine plan leading to peace, joy and fulfillment; and

3. Instead of the judgment of God, he receives God's blessing and promise of dwelling forever in heaven with him.

I'd say that is a pretty good ending for someone who was previously bound for destruction. Jesus has actually provided peace and wholeness for every part of our lives. Christ cares for the entire person as indicated in the following scripture passages:

"Now may the God of peace Himself sanctify you completely; and may your whole spirit, soul and body be preserved blameless at the coming of our Lord Jesus Christ." (1
Thessalonians 5:23)

&

"The thief comes only in order to steal and kill and destroy, I
came that they may have and enjoy life, and have it in abundance (to the full, till it overflows)." (John 10:10 AMP)

From his own mouth Jesus assures us that he does not

want us to remain as fragments (lives strewn in broken

pieces) or lost (spiritually dead, destroyed, marred or per-

ishing). Instead he wants us to be like those baskets men-

tioned in John 6:13—filled entirely with life and brimming

over. Thanks be to God! He is still sending out disciples to

gather up our fragmented lives through sharing the gospel

and reaching out to us with his love. As fragments we must

yield to his disciples' touch and allow ourselves to be gath-

ered up for the Lord. That means truly receiving the Good

News of Christ's substitutionary death by faith. It means

confessing Jesus as Lord and believing in our heart that God raised him from the dead after he was crucified for our sin. (See Romans 10:9-10). It also means allowing God to grow us up in his image by applying his Word that we learn through attending his church, studying the Bible, obeying the Holy Spirit and quickly repenting when we disobey.

As I stated before, our Christian walk is a process and the renewing of our mind takes time. Wrong thinking, bad motives and ideas have to be replaced by the character and will of God. The process of sanctification takes a lifetime requiring intimacy with the Lord and fellowship with other believers. Just like the gathering of the bread fragments took effort, so the gathering of people fragments will also take a two-fold painstaking effort on the part of believers. First, believers are called to share the message of Christ with all that they meet and secondly on a personal level each believer is commanded to be transformed by renewing their own minds through application of God's Holy Word. In this second command, God is essentially calling believers to gather up their

fragmented thoughts and to bring it into captivity unto the

obedience of Christ! Both parts of the assignment, reaching

the lost and renewing of our minds, can only be accomplished

with the help of the Holy Spirit and not by human effort

alone. In fact as the following scriptures indicate, this type

of transformation is only possible through the work of God:

> *But as many as received him, to them gave he power to*
> *become the sons of God, even to them that believe on*
> *his name: Which were born, not of the flesh, nor of the*
> *will of man, but of God.*   *John 1:12-13;*
> *[Jesus speaking] No man can come to me, except the*
> *Father which hath sent me draw him: and I will raise*
> *him up at the last day.*   *John 6:44*

&

> *That no flesh should glory in his presence. But of him*
> *are ye in Christ Jesus, who of God is made unto us*
> *wisdom, and righteousness, and sanctification, and*
> *redemption: that, according as it is written, He that glo-*
> *rieth, let him glory in the Lord.*
> *I Corinthians 1:29-31*

You'd think that all Christians having this knowl-

edge about the work of God would walk around feeling

pretty good and complete rather than feeling fragmented. Unfortunately, many Christians who have already received eternal life and freedom from the penalty of sin continue to live sad, fragmented lives because they remain fragmented in their thoughts. Disappointments and lack of discipline can sometimes make us lose sight of our self-worth and direction. We feel lost.

I felt lost for several years after my marriage failed. I couldn't fully appreciate my children, my family, health, gifts or even my relationship with my heavenly Father. I thought I would never laugh again or truly be joyful for more than a brief moment. I felt stuck, helpless, unlovely and unlovable. I couldn't reason my way out of these feelings, nor could my joy be sustained by the kind words

> *Though a Christian, I had a thought-life that was undisciplined by the Word of God. That was an awful place to be in because in that mindset I remained at the mercy of someone else's perception of me or at least their perception in my imagination and emotions.*

of others. Ultimately, I had to cry to the One who made me for help. I cried, "Help me Jesus! Your little sheep has fallen into a bitter pit and I can't get up out of here." He helped me by illuminating his Word to me and by helping me to recognize some of the wrong thoughts I had allowed to shape my self-image. At that point I realized that I had valued my self-worth based on what I imagined others thought of me rather than what God said about me in his Word. I had not learned to love myself and I was continually seeking validation.

Though a Christian, I had a thought-life that was undisciplined by the Word of God. That was an awful place to be in because in that mindset I remained at the mercy of someone else's perception of me or at least their perception in my imagination and emotions. Instead of the truth of God's Word dictating my actions and self-image, I was still allowing my emotions, the words or behavior of others and circumstances to define my thinking and my destiny. I had lived this way far too long. So I cried, "Lord, please help me to take authority over my thought life and show me my

purpose, my place and my value."

You may be wondering, "How in the world could someone

who is a born-again believer get such messed up thinking?"

Well, I'll tell you. Although I knew in my head that Jesus

loved me unconditionally and that I had value and purpose

in this world, I just couldn't let those truths permeate my

heart. Sometimes getting truth to travel the eighteen inches

from the head to the heart can take as long as the children

of Israel's journey from Egypt to the Promised Land. When

it should have taken only 11 days, their trip took 40 years

because of unbelief. They only got out of the wilderness

when the unbelieving negative talkers died off. Similarly,

when my circumstances helped drive me to a place of disci-

plining my thinking to fully believe and rehearse what God

says about me in the Bible and then to deliberately reject

the warped negative thoughts of victimization and low self-esteem, I too emerged from my wilderness into the healing and restorative power of God's grace.

I am glad the Lord has delivered me and freed me to share this hope with others. I am a witness that God's grace through faith in his son Jesus is sufficient to totally renew anyone's life and mind from being fragmented to becoming whole. The mind renewing part comes as I said from reading, believing and practicing the truth of God's word. This includes muzzling our mouths to stop practicing negative talk about ourselves and others. This can take a long time and ultimately a life-time. Old habits are hard to break, but the more we surrender to the work of the Holy Spirit, the more complete and fulfilled we will become.

The fragments also taught me the importance of gathering the nuggets of truth we learn along life's journey through victories and failures and placing them in the basket of our heart to share with others when the Holy Spirit gives us an opportunity. When the disciples picked up all the fragments, there were enough to fill twelve baskets to the state of brimming over. Some scholars indicate that these were twelve little hand baskets. Others believe the word transliterated as "hand basket" indicates how the baskets were made rather than the size of the basket. I don't know if each basket

> *Just as the fragments of bread and fish had to be gathered and stored in baskets for future use after the meal ended, so should the lessons the Lord teaches us be valued and stored in our memories to draw upon in the future.*

held three cups or three bushels of fragments. It really doesn't matter to me because as long as they had Jesus, whatever the amount, it was more than enough. The scripture indicates every single person including the disciples had eaten and was full from a miraculous meal prepared with 2 fish, 5 barley loaves and the blessing of Jesus. Then twelve hand baskets or bushel baskets of leftovers were gathered at the Lord's command so none of these fragments would go to waste. Why twelve? Since there were twelve baskets full there was enough for each of the Lords servants to have provision for later on.

Just as the fragments of bread and fish had to be gathered and stored in baskets for future use after the meal ended, so should the lessons the Lord teaches us be valued and stored in our memories to draw upon in the future. As you know, lessons can be learned through both positive and negative or joyful and painful experiences. The Lord expects us to appreciate all of his instructions, his blessings and his deliverances. He also intends for us to continually benefit from the valuable lessons we learned through often painful experiences we go through. This truth is reflected in the Proverbs:

Hear counsel, and receive instruction, that thou mayest be wise in thy latter end. There are many devices in a man's heart; nevertheless the counsel of the Lord, that shall stand. The fear of the Lord tendeth to life: and he that hath it shall abide satisfied; he shall not be visited with evil. Proverbs 19: 20-21, 23

The fact that the Lord tenderly manifests himself to us in these various ways helps us to trust him more and understand him better. Every time we get a new revelation of God's character in our lives, we have something more to add to our faith arsenal to counteract Satan's attacks. He does not want us to forget what he has done for us nor does he want us to ignore who he is to us.

The shepherd boy, David, experienced God's protection, empowerment and presence in his victorious battles with the lion and the bear. He spent long days and nights out in the field alone with God and the sheep. Each of his experiences enlarged his heart, his love and understanding of God. When he faced the giant, Goliath, in that fateful battle (I Samuel 17:12-51), he was sure of his own identity, God's presence and the covenant he had with God. He was then able to run with full confidence into the battle; drawing from God's word and the relationship he had developed with God to emerge victorious. God wants each of us to feast sufficiently on his provisions and to store up the remnants/ fragments to draw upon for future challenges as well. There is always going to be a new challenge that seems bigger and stronger than we are, but that is no reason for us to throw up our hands and shriek with despair. We are expected to remember, believe and act on that belief.

In our story about the loaves and fishes, we see that the disciples struggle with this process just like we do. They saw Jesus feed about fifteen thousand people with two fish and five loaves, but the bible said that a few hours later the disciples had already forgotten the miracle of the fish and the loaves because of the hardness of their hearts. (Mark 6:52). As a matter of fact, they were flabbergasted to see Jesus walking the waters and not believing their eyes they cried out, "It's a ghost!" They saw him as Lord over sickness, demons and even hunger, but to them that had nothing to do with being Lord over the elements. Similarly, we see Jesus as Lord in the church building, but find it difficult to see him as Lord in our homes with our teens, spouses and babies. He

knows about fish and stuff, but what could he possibly know

about Quantum Physics, business finance or a leaking hot

water tank? The Lord has given each of us basket-loads of

> *He not only can put things in our hands, but also teach us how to successfully use what is in our hands.*

blessing to demonstrate his love, character and ability, but we must guard our own hearts against spiritual hardening of

the arteries. After celebrating the blessing, he wants us to

remain confident in his goodness and in his ability to change

us and our lives. He works with us, for us and through us. He

not only can put things in our hands, but also teach us how to

successfully use what is in our hands.

Just as he told the disciples, "be not afraid it is I [or lit-

erally "I am; be not afraid]", he wants us to learn to stop

being afraid and to depend upon him as our source for every-

thing we need. The disciples learned about God's character

through positive experiences like the feeding of the five thousand men plus the women and children. The disciples also learned about God's character through negative experiences, too. Peter learned his own frailty and insufficiency when he denied Christ, but he also learned of his unfailing love and forgiveness when Jesus called for him after the Resurrection. I wish I could paint a beautiful picture of my own constant obedience and perfect faith, but it wouldn't be true.

God is merciful, but he also expects complete obedience whether the assignment seems hard or not. God had patiently worked with me, given me the tools and the encouragement to complete the assignment to write a book, but because I was afraid I hemmed and hawed about finishing it. He began sending more loving reminders through Christian brothers and sisters who told me that I needed to finish the job, but I politely silenced them by saying I was still working on it bit by bit. He began troubling my dreams. Then while preparing a sermon about the 'woman at the well' in John chapter 4. I read these words in John 4:34, "Jesus said to them, My food is to do the will of Him who sent Me and to **finish His work**.". The words seem to leap off of the page. Finish the book! That's what those three words seemed to shout. All that week I felt led to read about Gideon during my devotion time and every time I turned on the television or radio, I heard about how God transformed scared Gideon into a mighty man of valor. (See Judges 6-8). Then I started hearing the words, "My grace is sufficient for you, my strength is made perfect in your weakness" from 2 Corinthians 12:9 over and over in my head. God was trying to tell me, "You can do it! I will help you". Would you believe I still excused myself from pressing to finish the task? I reasoned that as long as I was doing a little along the way, I was within the will of God. Not! Yes, He understood my fears, but his grace and promises prove that fear is no excuse for disobedience.

God, being the wonderful parent that he is, warns us clearly that we are in disobedience, but he is also willing to do whatever is necessary to help us to amend our ways. Then it happened: within three days one thing after another began to break down to the point that I was stuck at home with no money and no transportation. Boy, God knows how to get our attention. I became quite motivated to repent and to get on the ball. He was only trying to get me into position to see him work a greater way in my life, but I was letting fear override the truth about the loving character of God. I knew that God loved me and was willing and able to help me be a victor in every situation, therefore, like David I should have run toward my Goliath, but I hadn't done it.

After I repented and purposed to fully obey God's instructions, suddenly the colossal seemed smaller. I had put my eyes back on God instead of myself and the challenge. It wasn't a pleasant experience, but I learned several valuable lessons from it. God wants to do and reveal more of himself to us but we must learn to treasure his blessings and to honor our relationship with him through trust and obedience. God wants us to gather all the fragments of truth we learn and also to be willing to share them. Actually, it is a real good idea to ask God when you are going through a storm to show you what he is trying to teach you so you don't have to repeat the process. Journaling sometimes helps me to analyze the situation more closely and helps me to remember. I don't know about you but I hate going through a bad time and then finding myself repeating it again before I get the message. Not only can we avoid the pain of repeating a training experience by remembering and sharing the lessons learned, but our learning experiences can even have a positive effect on someone close to us. Normally, we want to sweep bad experiences under the rug, but if we learned something valuable from the experience we should share that truth like we share the one learned from good experiences. The whole idea is that we gather up the fragments of blessings, people, truth, wisdom, joy, peace, and righteousness that remain so that none will be wasted or lost.

"Therefore, they gathered them together, and filled twelve baskets with the fragments of the five barley loaves, which remained over and above unto them that had eaten" (John 6:13). In that verse, the word "remain" means: 1) to super abound in quantity or quality, 2) to be in excess, 3) to cause to excel, make more, and 4) to be the better, enough and to spare. Did you know that God never allows suffering to go to waste in the life of a believer? Even negative experiences that were our own fault can work together for our good making us stronger and to become better encouragers of someone else, like our children. For instance, if I recognize mistakes I made in judgment regarding a business decision or dangerous warning signs I ignored in an abusive relationship, but I don't share them because I am embarrassed about my foolishness, my child may fall into the same mess because I didn't warn them. Sometimes you can warn a child and he may still repeat the mistake, but transparency about God's grace in even a bad situation may help to steer your child or friend toward following God's plan. In that way even the bad can work out for someone else's good.

When we repent and the Lord delivers us, rather than hiding our mistakes and denying our bad choices, we can help our children avoid the same pitfalls by sharing the lessons we learned. "Often common sins or weaknesses seem to run in a family and it is called a generational curse."[1] How many times have you seen patterns of teen pregnancy, divorce, infidelity, abuse, incest, jail and drug use in families? We call them generational curses and indeed they are. It is the curse of un-confronted, unexposed or unrepentant iniquity in our hearts that is perpetuated from one generation to the next. As mentioned in Numbers 14:18, "The Lord is longsuffering and of great mercy, forgiving iniquity and transgression, and by no means clearing the guilty, visiting the iniquity of the fathers upon the children unto the third and fourth generation."

A lot of the same mistakes can be avoided and the curse can be broken by mom and grandma honestly sharing from a repentant heart, the lessons they learned the hard way with daughter and granddaughter. Dad can help son keep from getting entangled with the addiction to pornography if he will only confess the painful lessons learned before he was delivered. Satan gets a thrill at seeing us and our families falter over and over again. Pride tells us to keep our short-comings to ourselves and many times our kids fall into the same disastrous ditch we just climbed out of. Proverbs warns us that, "Pride goes before destruction, and a haughty spirit before a fall" (Proverbs 16:18). What is more painful than to see your child endure the same heartaches you endured?

Here is a case of just such a generational curse:

A mom remains in an abusive marriage not requiring her husband to treat her with dignity and respect and then later grows old, bitter and disrespectful herself. The girl children witness his behavior and her attitude and vow they will never take such mess off of a man. Instead of surrendering their own marriages to God, the adult females develop unhealthy trust issues and may view divorce as the cure-all at the first sign of any marital problems. Most of the time that marriage and maybe even another will fail due to this unhealthy mindset. Then the stage is set to repeat the cycle for yet another unhealthy relationship during the next gen-eration because the children from the broken home vow to be willing to take anything rather than put their children through the pangs of divorce.

On the other hand the male children often view abuse and infidelity as a sign of masculinity and therefore also develop an unhealthy attitude toward a marriage relationship. The same behavior is often carried out in their marriages causing a perpetuation of the cycle. He may feel emasculated and full of rage if his wife refuses to tolerate such behavior. Each of these marriage cycles could be avoided or the marriages could have been repaired if there had been confession of wrong motives and a deliberate commitment to love each other God's way. "Above all things have fervent love for one another, for love will cover a multitude of sins," (I Peter 4:8). Also, I am convinced that fewer relationships would be lost – become ruined, destroyed or go astray – if more of us would dare to gather and stand on the inerrant truths of God's Word regardless to how we feel and if we would honestly strive to admit when we miss the mark. This would require commitment on the part of both the men and women to seek God's help through prayer and honest application of the biblical principles concerning the roles of husbands and wives in marriage.

Of course, there is no guarantee that our children will not make the same mistakes we did, but if we humbly share our mistakes and the truths learned from God's Word there is a better chance that they will be successful in their lives. "… Yes, all of you be submissive to one another, and be clothed with humility, for God resists the proud, But gives grace to the humble". (I Peter 5:5)

Certainly, I find it much easier to paint the picture that I have never erred, especially to a generation who was not there to witness my blunders, but the price is far too high. James 1:9 says that "If we confess our sins, he is faithful and just and will forgive our sins and cleanse us from all unrighteousness." Though it is uncomfortable, I find the Lord helps me to share with my own children blunders I have made in order to aid them in making better choices. If each of us examined our lives, we would be able to gather up so many fragments to share from the truth of God's Word and his loving grace shown toward us that it would be more than enough to suffice for this and future generations. Christ has a way of changing everything that comes through his hands, even what may seem to others like useless fragments. So, let the Lord teach you how to gather up the fragments around and within you so that you might lose none.

Jesus Doesn't Skip Women and Children

Chapter 12

And they did all eat, and were filled: and they took up of the fragments that remained twelve baskets full. And they that had eaten were about five thousand men, beside women and children. Matt.14:20-21

A t the conclusion of this marvelous miracle of the fishes and the loaves, all four of the Gospel writers focused on the facts that 1) everyone ate and everyone was filled, 2) twelve baskets of leftover fragments were gathered and 3) a record number of five thousand men were fed. In Matthew's gospel, he also mentions an enormous though unnumbered group of women and children in the multitude that was fed in that desert place. I think it is important to ponder the question as to why were twelve baskets of fragments collected that evening. Then we will look at the importance of Matthew's commentary about the large group of women and children present on the scene beside those five thousand men.

First, it seems interesting that there were exactly twelve baskets full of fragments collected and only the twelve disciples got into the boat that evening to cross the sea. Because Jesus remained alone on the shore to pray, there were obviously enough baskets of food in the ship so each man could have his own. Ultimately they were going to toil at sea for hours before Jesus arrived walking the waters in the wee hours of the morning and they would need sustenance for the journey ahead. (See Mark 6:45-51) The thought reminds me of those tasty picnic baskets of fried chicken and goodies mama packed for our family when we prepared to make that long 16-hour drive between Chicago and New Orleans when

I was young. Mama made sure we were fully prepared during the long trip. Similarly, the Lord knew what was looming ahead in the disciples' future and he made sure there was enough to sustain each of them for the trip and the hardship ahead. He still does the same thing for us. I think, if we take the time to reflect on the many things God has already brought us through, the loving grace and new tender mercies he gives us each and every day, not to mention the Bible road map he provided, we would discover that we have enough truth and grace to sustain us for whatever is up ahead in our journey as well.

When I went through a time of intense depression and questioning of my identity because of the abuse and humiliation suffered in my life, the Lord sustained me by positioning key people in my life to encourage and build me up during some of my roughest periods. God often encouraged me through friends and honors on the job when my self-esteem and self-worth were being eroded at home. When I was deserted and rejected by my husband, I received tender love from my children, mom and siblings. Then to my surprise, the Lord gave me even more sisters and brothers in Christ who loved me and helped to show me my value in God's kingdom. When I look back, I realize that God had me covered at all times and on all sides no matter what threatened my existence. Even when we do not realize his presence and his provision, he is busy caring for us in a multitude of undeserved ways.

Despite the fact that God's providential provision is a marvelous subject, the gospel writers pointed out the twelve baskets for reasons beyond the disciples' dietary sustenance. In fact, the number twelve represented a signpost that pointed to the establishment of a new kingdom on earth—God's Kingdom. The number twelve announced that the foundations of God's Kingdom had been laid and established. In the Bible and Hebrew history several numbers have significance and are used repeatedly or in multiples all throughout

Scripture, i.e. the numerals 1, 3, 4, 6, 7, 10, 12, 40, 70, and

1000. For example, the number one usually represents unity

as it was used in reference to the union of a man and woman

in marriage (Genesis 2:24), God himself announced the fact

that He, the Triune God, is One (Deuteronomy 6:4) when he

gave the Ten Commandments and Jesus stated that he and

the Father are one as he prayed for unity among the believers

(John 17:20-21). It is generally understood in scripture that

six is the number of man (Revelation 13:18) and the number

seven represents completion or perfection in scripture as it is

often used to represent God's perfect holiness, knowledge,

wisdom, power, etc. (see Zechariah 4:10 and Revelation

1:4). However, according to some bible scholars, the number

twelve is often associated with divine administration, estab-

lishment and the elective purposes of God for his people.

Also, the Hebrew calendar has 12 months and their day is

divided into twelve hours. (See Esther 3:7; John 11:9), The

bible has many other passages linking the number twelve

with divine administration and establishment. The Lord promised that he would make or establish Abram as a great nation saying Abraham's seed would be established to be as great as the dust of the earth and stars of the sky. When God established that Abraham would be the father of many nations, he told Abraham that Ishmael was not the promised seed, but for Abraham's sake he would establish him as a great nation, giving him twelve sons or princes (Genesis 17:20). From Abraham's grandson Jacob whose name was later changed to Israel, God brought forth and preserved throughout history the twelve tribes of Israel from which the King of Kings would be born.

Following the birth of Jesus, the Scriptures note that at the age of twelve, he declared his mission. When he had thoroughly confounded the scribes and Pharisees with his understanding of the Law, he announced to his parents that He was all about doing 'His Father's business'. Unfortunately, they didn't know what he meant (Luke 2:42-50). However, throughout his brief 3 and 1/2 years of ministry, Jesus made

his business perfectly clear. Prior to the feeding of the five

thousand, Jesus announced that the kingdom of God had

come and that he, the Lord of Lords, had arrived to establish

it.

Now after that John was put in prison, Jesus came into Galilee, preaching the gospel of the kingdom of God, And saying, The time is fulfilled, and the kingdom of God is at hand: repent ye, and believe the gospel. Mark 1:14-15

&

The Spirit of the Lord is upon me, because he hath anointed me to preach the gospel to the poor he hath sent me to heal the brokenhearted, to preach deliverance to the captives, and recovering of sight to the blind, to set at liberty them that are bruised, to preach the acceptable year of the Lord. And he began to say unto them. This day is this scripture fulfilled in your ears. Luke 4:18-19, 21

After carefully spelling out his mission to establish the

Kingdom of God, Jesus beautifully painted a picture of the

Kingdom through sermons, parables and lengthy teachings

like the "sermon on the mount" and those he taught on the

seaside of Galilee. Then he also demonstrated his kingdom

and his authority through miracles, healing, deliverance and

by the appointing of the twelve apostles. The Twelve, as they

were often referred to, were commissioned to go throughout

the world laying the foundation of the church—faith in the

Name of Jesus, the Christ...

> *Now therefore ye are no more strangers and foreigners,*
> *but fellowcitizens with the saints, and of the household*
> *of God; And are built upon the foundations of the apos-*
> *tles and prophets, Jesus Christ himself being the chief*
> *cornerstone. Ephesians 2:19-20*

From Genesis to Revelation, there is much use of the

number twelve in association with the establishment of

God's will in the earth. When looking at a picture of the

Kingdom of Heaven in the book of Revelation, the number

twelve and multiples of twelve are used to represent God's

people and the description of the heavenly city, the place pre-

pared for God's people. For instance, there is a reference to the 144,000 as representing those sealed to witness through the earth from the twelve tribes of Israel. There is also mention of the twelve gates of the city containing the names of the tribes, the twelve foundations bearing the names of the apostles, and to the trees bearing twelve crops of fruit signifying the never-ending abundance and life in the Kingdom of God (See Revelation 7:3-4, 21:12-14 & 22:2)

I think it is no coincidence that just prior to the miracle of the loaves and the fishes, it is recorded that Jesus heals a woman who had an issue of blood for twelve years and raises the Jewish ruler Jairus' daughter from the dead, who was (you guessed it) *twelve* years old. (See Luke 8:41-56). I believe these miracles were signposts pointing to the establishment of the Kingdom and demonstrating that Jesus, God's Son, has authority over all sin, sickness, death, poverty and hopelessness. The miracle of feeding five thousand men with five loaves and two fishes and then having *twelve* baskets full of fragments remaining established his authority over hunger and over every need of man. The twelve bas-

kets signaled that the all-sufficient kingdom of God and

the authority of the Bread of Life have been established on

Earth. It reminds me that by faith his all-sufficient, loving

and righteous Kingdom reigns in and is established in my

life and the life of every man, woman and child who believes

in him.

These miracles established that: yes, Jesus is Lord over

sickness, disease, poverty, death, and sin but also, that he

is actively involved in the rescuing of women and children.

Jesus restored the life and wholeness to Jarius' twelve-year-

old child. When everyone else said the child's father was

wasting the Lord's time because the girl was too far gone,

Jesus told the father to keep believing and he would see his

child healed. When others laughed at Jesus when he said the

girl was sleeping and not dead, he proved that he alone had

the final say concerning the child's life. Christ cares about all people, all ages and in any condition. We are never beyond his reach or his ability to change our situations and us.

When Jesus arrived and took charge, the hopeless situation was thoroughly changed. The dead girl became alive and well. She sat up and was able to receive nourishment for her newly resurrected body. The girl's formerly heartbroken parents were now full of joy and thanksgiving because the Lord himself had come to see about them. The Scriptures tell us that Jesus also told the parents to give the child something to eat after he resurrected her. I believe that reference was another reminder of the loving care God has for children. He knew the parents did not know how best to care for the child who had just been brought back into the land of the living. The parents needed instruction because they might have become preoccupied with celebrating the miracle or they may have spent a long time staring at the child in amazement. Jesus knew the restored body needed to be nourished and he told the parents as much. Likewise, many parents do not know how to properly care for their children today, but the Lord will guide us if we will listen to him as these parents did. Truly Jesus had established that God alone has the last word and that he can do anything, but fail.

The woman with the issue of blood was desperately weak, helpless and rejected because of her blood loss. The law labeled her as unclean. The scripture says she grew worse at the hand of the physicians and she became lonely and financially impoverished because of her condition. She had been sick for twelve long years. The woman was established as hopelessly unclean and waiting for death. The fact that she touched Jesus while he was on his way to his care for Jairus' ailing daughter may have appeared to some as an interruption and most certainly a violation of the Law. But all of these negatives did not put her off limits to the healing touch of Christ. She only had to reach out by faith and to believe that he would heal her completely and she was instantly healed.

Gender, age, status or race do not move the hand of the Master. Faith in God moves him! "But without faith it is impossible to please him: for he that cometh to God must believe that he is and that he is a rewarder of them that diligently seek him." (Hebrews 11:6)

Going from being a married, respected pastor's wife, minister and mother, to a divorced, humiliated, depressed, broke and displaced middle-aged minister and mother left me feeling much like the woman with the issue of blood. I had stayed under stress and abuse far too long and it had drained out my hope and self-worth. It felt like I was permanently doomed to hopelessness. The emotional burdens had taken a toll on my health as well. I couldn't sleep and my hair continued to fall out. I found myself feeling unclean like the woman and helplessly dead like the little girl. By the grace of God and through faith in Jesus' goodness and mercy, his authority and power overcame my circumstances. Jesus resurrected my life and my identity.

I am so glad the Holy Spirit comforted me and paid close attention to everything that concerned me. God never lets even one of us slip through the cracks of life uncared for. He is actually concerned about every minute detail of our lives. For that reason, I believe he caused the apostle Matthew, a former tax collector, to also develop a keen eye for detail. His account of this miracle is the only one that included the detail that there were more than just men present in the crowd that day. I am so glad the Lord had him to add the words, "beside the women and the children"!

Certainly five thousand was a miraculous number of people to be fed off of one tiny lunch basket containing two fish and five small barley loaves. But, considering Matthews statement, there could have been as many as fifteen thousand people fed that day instead of only five thousand assuming the men had brought along their families. During that day, it was customary for men and women to eat separately. In fact, the 21ˢᵗ Century edition of the Strongest Strong's Exhaustive

Concordance of the Bible states that the Greek word translated "beside" in this verse means "by itself, separately, apart from, or independent from". Perhaps that separation was the reason Mark, Luke and John did not mention the women and children in their headcount even though they were also fed. Most likely, however, they were not mentioned because in their patriarchal culture, men were the only ones counted when taking a census.

The fact that the Holy Spirit impressed upon Matthew to include the detail that Jesus fed women and children as well, reminds us that God's grace is available to all and his Kingdom supersedes societal rules and restrictions. In that culture and some cultures today, women and children were subordinate and generally viewed as a man's cherished possessions. According to Philo, a Jewish writer and philosopher who lived during the time of this miracle, there were certain roles allowed or limited by a person's gender. In fact, it was considered immodest for women to be involved in or even party to open air discussions:

> Market places, council chambers and courts of justice and large companies...crowds, and life in the open air full of arguments and actions relating to war and peace, are suited to men; but taking care of the house and remaining at home are the proper duties of women... (p. 611, Philo – The Special laws III)

However, Philo stated that virtuous women were pious, selfless and diligent in their service to God and for this reason he thought, Moses allowed them to be involved in the sacred work of preparing the Tabernacle:

> On which count Moses also committed the preparation of the sacred works of the tabernacle not only to men, but also to women, who were to aid in making them; for all "the woven works of hyacinthine colour, and of purple and of scarlet work and of fine linen, and of goats' hair, do the women make;" and they also contribute their own ornaments without hesitation... [p. 262, Works of Philo, On the Migration of Abraham, (97)]

Josephus, the famous Jewish historian, stated that the testimony of a woman wasn't even allowed by members of his sect in trials. Women were considered silly and rash: *"But let not the testimony of women be admitted, on account of the levity and boldness of their sex..."* |p. 117, The Works of Josephus, 1980|. Philo considered children as possessions or highly favored servants because they had to be expensively cared for by their parents.

> But parents have received not only the power of ruler and governor over their children but ...master, according to both the very highest of characteristics of possession of servants...who by the laws of nature receive from the masters of the house a sufficient support to maintain them in life after they are born. (p.590, The Works of Philo, 1993).

I am glad Jesus does not devalue, overlook or limit a person because of gender or age, but instead consistently demonstrates that everyone matters to God— including women and children. Christ's arrival established a new just way of doing things. In God's economy, he blesses the children for he said, "of such is the kingdom of heaven" and he makes a memorial of the woman who courageously poured

out her love to him before his crucifixion. The condition
of the heart is what matters to God. For Jesus brought his
kingdom and salvation to the hearts of men, women and
children by grace through faith in his name. No one is a
second-class citizen in the Kingdom of God:

> *There is neither Jew nor Greek, there is neither bond*
> *nor free, there is neither male nor female: for ye are all*
> *one in Christ Jesus. And if ye be Christ's, then are ye*
> *Abraham's seed, and heirs according to the promise.*
> *Galatians 3:28-29*

The Lord God has continually condemned mistreatment
of women and children throughout history. In both the Old
Testament and the New, the Scriptures clearly teach that children are to be nurtured, taught and trained. Women are to be
honored and treated as the weaker or precious vessels. They
are also to be protected and well cared for by their fathers
until given in marriage to a husband who will cherish her
as he does his own body. He sees and gravely disapproves
of the worldwide injustice of human trafficking. The Lord

counts our faith as being more valuable than gold, whether we are male, female, adult or child. In fact, when people honor God by placing him first in their households, there will be a positive impact on their spouses, their children and their communities with God's presence, provision, guidance and protection.

We may never know exactly how many women and kids were there that evening, but the effect this miracle had on that countless number for many years is mind-boggling. As all of them witnessed the creative power of Jesus Christ and heard Him expound on the Kingdom of God, possibly over fifteen thousand people were exposed to the living Word of God in one afternoon even without the benefit of television, radio or the Internet. These people took what they saw and heard to their homes and their communities. It works the same today. Imagine if every man in our community brought their family to church to learn about and to worship Jesus Christ and then went home and lived by God's principles. What an over-whelming impact would be made on our society!

The lives of millions would be saved and changed. We would undoubtedly have a safer, giving and more loving community. The kingdom of God would reign in our country and we would be even more blessed as a nation. Business practices would no longer be focused on profit more than on people. The jails would not be over-run with frustrated, angry young men and women. More women and men would be married and raising God-fearing children in a two-parent heterosexual home. God-loving responsible fathers and husbands living according to God's guidelines found in the Scriptures would greatly reduce the epidemic of absentee fathers. The number of desperate murders to unwanted babies would drastically decrease. The need for acceptance in gangs would diminish. Young men and women would not need to try to find love in all the wrong places. With Christ giving changing us from the inside out and giving our lives purpose, holy men and women would be empowered to stand victoriously against drugs, pornography, etc. We need Christ in our lives and therefore it is critically important that everyone has an opportunity to hear and understand the gospel message: "For God so loved the world that he gave his only begotten Son, that whosoever believeth in him should not perish but shall have everlasting life" (John 3:16). Unfortunately, everyone will not receive the message of Christ before he returns because Satan is so very deceitful and because the bible says that men love darkness rather than light. However, that fact should not deter us from trying to reach as many as we can for him.

In view of all the thoughts we have discussed regarding the multitude and the twelve baskets, I believe its safe to say that numbers matter to God. But we also should never under estimate the value and power of one person who receives and really believes the message of Christ. If it wasn't for one little unnamed boy who generously donated his lunch by faith, there would have been no miracle of the fish and loaves that evening. God could have rained down manna and quail, but in his kingdom he has chosen to use us who will obey him by faith. Undoubtedly, the young boy had heard the words of Christ when he expounded on how he should live if he believed in Jesus and was a part of the Kingdom. He must have believed and applied the words of Jesus when he said, "Give to every man that asketh of thee... And as ye would that men should do to you, do ye also to them like-wise." (Luke 6:30-31) The little boy heard, believed and acted on what Jesus said. As a result, a child is credited with being used by the Lord in the feeding of the masses. Matthew mentioned the women and the children in his account of this miracle, but we would not have known of the little boy's contribution and his act of faith, if John, the youngest of the twelve, had not mentioned him in his account. Each one of the gospel writers added a valuable part to the gospel message contained in this miracle's account. The little boy made a huge difference that day.

From the beginning of time until now, the Lord has shown us the importance of just one person's obedience or disobedience. One man, Adam, caused death to reign in the lives of all men because of sin and disobedience. Through the faithfulness of one man, Abraham, his seed obtained the promise of being the people of God. And finally, through the obedience of the God-man, Jesus Christ, we can obtain deliverance from the bondage of sin and death to the glorious liberty of forgiveness and life eternal by faith in His Name. One child, one man or one woman can make a difference!

In the Bible, one woman, Deborah led Israel to victory over their enemies because she dared to believe and obey God. In more recent history, Jane Addams, being moved by God's compassion, founded Hull house for poor immigrant workers families, co-founded the NAACP, impacted national child labor laws and won the Nobel Peace Prize. She was one person who acted on faith and greatly impacted many worldwide. Mary McLeod Bethune is another courageous woman who could have allowed herself to be hindered by racial prejudice and poverty, but her faith in God prompted her to act on the behalf of uneducated black children. She used her gift as an educator and despite tremendous opposition started and maintained a school for African American girls. It eventually became co-ed Bethune-Cookman College. Mrs. Bethune was chosen by United States presidents to advise on National minority and youth advisory councils, to assist the secretary of war during WWII and also received the international Medal of Honor from Haiti. One woman trusted God, poured herself out and impacted thousands. Who can ignore the unselfish and tireless service of love given by Mother Teresa to comfort countless thousands of poor, sick, hopeless and dying people in the streets of Calcutta, India? Her selfless devotion prompted by the compassion of Christ caused her to begin a new Catholic order that now ministers to AIDS victims in Africa and to the Poor on six continents. She also received the Nobel Peace Prize. All these great people demonstrated the difference one can make if we by faith pour ourselves out for the sake of the kingdom and for others.

The young boy's act of placing the loaves and fishes in Jesus' hand symbolized his overwhelming desire to please the Master and his total trust in Christ's ability to use what he had to offer. Likewise the Lord wants us to exhibit that same level of commitment to his kingdom and trust in his power to use us. His act of generosity caused him to be blessed and to become a huge blessing to the men, the women and to the other children. God wants to do the same thing with our lives. He wants us to realize the great difference we can make if we by faith pour ourselves out for the sake of the kingdom and for others.

To start with, we can make a huge difference if we would apply our faith and dare to give ourselves away in our own homes. When the former demon-possessed man known in the Bible as "Legion" because of his many demons received the tender mercies of God, he was thoroughly set free by Christ. He then desired to cling to Jesus and requested to travel with him and the Twelve. But Jesus told him: *"Go home to your friends, and tell them what great things the Lord has done for you and how he has had compassion on you."* Mark 5:19. I believe the Lord wants us to pour out the fragments of praise about God's goodness and honestly share what God has delivered us from to help our family, friends and everyone we meet. It means sharing successes, mistakes and failures in light of the Word of God. Proving that God's Kingdom has been established in our hearts may help others choose to live their lives by faith in Jesus Christ and in obedience to his holy Word.

The most important thing to remember is that even though our lives represent only a morsel of God's Kingdom, the glory of the fragment rest in the hands of the Master. The loaves and the fishes a few hours earlier were just ordinary groceries, but they became useful tools for the Lord to do far more than their natural potential when they rested in Jesus' hands. Instead of satisfying the hunger of one little boy, these few fish and five loaves fed over five thousand folks. As the loaves and fishes had no natural ability within themselves to bless so many neither do we. Only as we dwell, rest in and remain connected to Jesus can we produce so much and bless so many.

The most important thing to remember is that even though our lives represent only a morsel of God's Kingdom, the glory of the fragment rest in the hands of the Master.

About the Author

Reverend Cynthia Hill

R ev. Cynthia Hill is the pastor of Joy River Baptist Church, a wonderful fellowship in Elgin, Illinois. She was licensed to preach in May 1998 at Logan Street Missionary Baptist Church of Batavia, IL. Later she received two years of invaluable training and serving as a minister of the First Cathedral in Bloomfield, CT. under Bishop LeRoy Bailey. The Lord led her to return to Illinois where God allowed her ministry to blossom under the leadership and training of Rev. Nathaniel L. Edmond, pastor of Second

Baptist Church of Elgin. Pastor Edmond ordained her in July 2006 and remains her pastor and mentor. Rev. Hill has a Bachelor of Arts Degree from Northeastern Illinois University and educational training from Spelman College, University of Chicago and Elgin Community College. Her additional Biblical training and education was received from The New England School of Ministry, the Progressive National Baptist Convention's Institute, Precepts Ministry Leaders Institute, ministry training seminars and consistent bible study. Rev. Hill has served in pastoral ministry, youth ministry, Christian education, prison ministry, counseling & biblical studies counselor at the Coventry House for Women in Connecticut. She has been blessed to encourage others through national conference speaking and singing.

Prior to full-time ministry, her twenty year professional career at First Card Credit Services of Elgin helped to hone her skills in leadership and communication. Beginning in an entry-level position in customer service, she served as a supervisor, team lead, training facilitator and human resource coordinator. Through the blessings of God she received many friends, growth experiences and awards of leadership and diversity during her years of service.

Although she went through an extremely challenging time, when her marriage of nearly 29 years came to an end, God revitalized and reshaped her into a dynamic and joyful vessel that celebrates life in Jesus. She is a proud grandmother of six grandchildren and the mother of four magnificent children who are Spirit-filled servants of Jesus Christ. God has graciously blessed them as pastor's kids to develop a deep love for Christ, ministry and education, which they have interwoven into their own professional careers.

Rev. Hill finds nothing more fulfilling than teaching and preaching God's word to all ages with the purpose of promoting faith in the matchless name of Jesus Christ. As pastor of Joy River Baptist Church, she has been blessed to labor with other loving Christians toward fulfilling the vision of evangelism and restoration. Although the fellowship is small this Church celebrates with joy the love of Christ boldly sharing the message of salvation, deliverance, encourage-ment, spiritual growth and holy living in Jesus Christ. Being personally acquainted with victory born through adversity, Rev. Hill encourages women, men and children with the statement that, "God loves you and has a wonderful plan for your life!" Since her conversion at the age of fourteen, she has boldly proclaimed her love for Jesus Christ and her dedication to the Gospel message of reconciliation to any and everyone who would hear.

As a witness to the transforming power of the Holy Spirit in the life of all who learn to trust, obey and depend upon the Name of Christ, she heralds the call to present your body as a living sacrifice to God and be transformed by the renewing of your mind through God's Word! Romans 12:1-2

REFERENCES

Johnson, V.L., (1995). <u>Restoring Broken Vessels</u>. Detroit, MI: Dabar Publishing Co.

Strong, J., Swanson, J.A. & Kohlenberger, J.R., III (2001). <u>The Strongest Strong's Exhaustive Concordance of the Bible</u>. Grand Rapids, MI: Zondervan.

Unger, M. F. & Severance, W. M (2007). <u>Unger's Concise Bible Dictionary with Complete Pronunciation Guide to Bible Names.</u> Grand Rapids, MI: Baker Book House.

Vine, W. E., Unger, M.F. & White, W., Jr. (1985). <u>Vine's Complete Expository Dictionary of Old and New</u>

Testament Words. Nashville, TN, Thomas Nelson Inc.

The Works of Philo Complete and Unabridged. [Trans. Charles Duke Yonge; new updated version; Peabody, MA: Henrickson Publisher's, Inc., 1993]

The Works of Josephus Complete and Unabridged. [Trans. William Whiston; new updated edition; Peabody, MA: Henrickson Publisher's, Inc., 1987]

CPSIA information can be obtained
at www.ICGtesting.com
Printed in the USA
LVOW12s2341300317
529133LV00001B/39/P